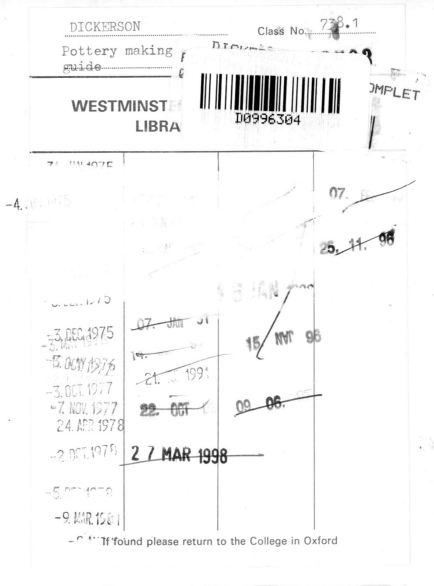

POTTERY MAKING
A COMPLETE GUIDE

John Dickerson

Nelson

This book was designed and produced by
George Rainbird Ltd
Marble Arch House, 44 Edgware Road, London W2

Published in Great Britain in 1974 by
Thomas Nelson and Sons Ltd
36 Park Street, London W1

House Editor: Erica Hunningher
Designer: Pauline Harrison
Index by Myra Clark

Colour plates originated by Cox & Wyman Ltd, Fakenham, Norfolk

Text printed and bound by A. Wheaton & Company, Exeter

ISBN: 0 17 141038 X

Reverse of frontispiece Chinese Tz'u-chou ware. Thrown
pot with brushwork decoration. Height approx. 10 in. (254 mm).
Eumorfapoulos Collection, Victoria & Albert Museum,
London. Photo: P. Macdonald

Frontispiece Stoneware sculpture by Jill Crowley. Luted
construction from moulded forms. Height approx. 16 in. (406 mm).
Photo: P. Macdonald

Contents

Contents

Introduction

The making of pottery is a uniquely appealing activity, for it offers a breadth of experience unrivalled among all the other arts. The pure kinaesthetic pleasure of throwing on the potter's wheel; the opportunity to synthesize the arts of sculpture and painting; the chance to explore whole themes in the time it would take the painter to prepare his canvas – these are among its more obvious attractions. But pottery has more than this obvious appeal. A rich source of material for self-discovery and self-development is made available to even the casual amateur, while deeper insights are the reward for more devoted involvement. The art is unique in that it throws us into an intimate relationship with nature – we have to establish a rapport with some of her primary forces, earth and water, air and fire. Pottery turns man back to nature to discover basic laws and to experience the disciplines and rhythms of natural process, in the face of which we have to question our own thought processes, attitudes and tastes, put our integrity to the test and constantly reassess our values.

Finally, it is refreshing to think that an activity which is so rich in potential is essentially available to all who wish to explore it. While some kinds of pottery do make use of expensive equipment and rare materials the majority of processes can be followed quite cheaply and some techniques involve no financial outlay at all.

While great pots may be as demanding to produce as great poems or symphonies, they are still essentially simple things, close to the earth and emblematic of their maker. If you aspire to produce only humble forms or if you decide to concentrate on the production of functional pieces you can yet be sure that the practice of pottery will enrich your sensitivities, broaden your insights and bring you close to the mainstream of one of man's oldest and most universal creative activities.

1 Clay

Ceramic is probably the most durable material in which the artist or artisan has ever couched his ideas. Pottery articles, even those dating back three thousand years or more, retain their original detail of form, brightness and surface qualities. Although ceramic articles are comparatively easily broken the material itself is virtually indestructible. Pieces of pottery have outlasted seemingly stronger materials such as stone and metal, largely because pottery is able to withstand the effects of atmospheric acids and other corrosive agents. Most materials available to the artist which offer durability as one of their characteristics, such as metal, are laborious to work and relatively insensitive to the hand that seeks to give them form. One of the greatest attractions of pottery is that while it is strong, rigid and durable in the fired state it is highly malleable, uniquely responsive to the artist's touch and generally easy to work throughout the formation stages.

Although we are aware of the changes of seasons and the passage of years we tend to think that these affect only the surface of our planet and that the earth below has a kind of eternal permanence. This idea may satisfy a psychological desire for security but, of course, it is highly erroneous. The planet is, as it always has been, in a constant state of flux.

The landscape that we see in the context of our short lives as unchanging and seemingly immutable represents but one stage in a vastly longer process of modification. In its geological infancy the earth was composed of a molten mass of matter beneath a very thin frozen skin. Within this fluid mass a separation of the denser materials and the less dense tended to occur, the former sinking to lower levels, the latter remaining nearer the surface. With the subsequent cooling of the earth a thicker crust of igneous rock was formed which probably had a fairly high degree of homogeneity over the whole globe. Geochemically three-quarters of this lithosphere is composed of silica and alumina while materials deriving from iron, sodium, magnesium, potassium and titanium form the bulk of the remainder. The earth minerals which were crystallized through the cooling process, due to local conditions and various local interactions, gave rise at certain points in the crust to such familiar forms as feldspar, quartz and iron-magnesium minerals. In the millennia following its formation, the igneous crust underwent massive modification through natural mechanics and chemical reaction. Rocks were split through stresses of expansion and contraction and surfaces were eroded by weathering and glaciation. The physical effects of water together with the solubility of some of the earth's constituents played an important part in the process of transfiguration, as did the decomposing effects of acids. All these and other processes played their part in breaking down the original form of the crust while some of them contributed to the further process of transporting and mixing the fractured mineral particles that erosion had created. Thus, much of the earth's surface has been broken down to be deposited again, either on-site or elsewhere, as sediment. Often these strata have been transformed yet again by hydrolysis or, subjected to pressure or heat, new metamorphic forms have emerged; these, too, have been attacked and fragmented by the relentless processes of erosion.

Among the earth minerals which have been formed and finally deposited out of this vast and on-going evolution one of the most common is clay. Basically, clay is the result of the hydrolysis of eroded fragments of feldspathic rock, although subject to local chemical variations, it is normally considered to exist in a pure form as the mineral kaolinite whose chemical formula is:

$$Al_2O_3 . 2SiO_2 . 2H_2O$$

The characteristics of clay can be divided into two categories, physical and chemical. Both are the concern of the potter and ideally there should be no division in his understanding of the two; the manipulation of the one should intuitively respond to the demands of the other. However, in learning about pottery it is useful to consider the two aspects of clay separately in the first instance.

The physical possibilities of clay as a creative material

PLASTICITY   In practical terms the attraction of clay is its malleability, the fact that it faithfully records the imprint of forces brought to bear upon it and responds in the most positive way to the form-giving hand. This receptivity to being shaped, and the subsequent retention of the given shape upon drying, is known as 'plasticity'. Because of its plasticity clay can be pulled up into high thin-walled forms without tearing or subsequent slumping. It allows a shape once formed to be radically modified or indeed totally altered without collapse or disintegration and, further, it allows satellite forms such as handles, spouts or high relief decoration to be welded on to the parent mass and to retain this positive adhesion as the clay stiffens and dries.

The plasticity of clay depends on three simple factors; of these, the most significant is a direct extension of the physical form of the individual clay particle. Clay is composed of myriad particles and, although some are comparatively large in size and irregular in shape, the overwhelming majority are flat, slab-like, polished crystalline particles of extreme minuteness. When clay is dug in its raw state from the earth it is frequently dense and rock-like in appearance except that it breaks easily and surfaces tend to powder in the hands. However, when this clay has been suitably impregnated with pore water each flat constituent particle becomes coated with a thin lubricating film that allows smooth fluid movement to take place within the mass between the faces of the particles. This extreme mobility within the same plane is coupled with a remarkable resistance to being torn apart against the direction of alignment. In both the malleable and dry states the overlap of many thousands of these lamellar particles imparts a high degree of mechanical strength to the material.

The shape and size of the individual clay particle is not the sole factor that determines plasticity; this is also influenced by the degree of ionization within the pore water (which acts as an electrolyte) together with some electro-chemical attraction between the particles themselves.

Finally, bacteria and other microscopic organisms present within the clay serve further to improve its workability by releasing colloidal fluids into the pore water.

The degree of plasticity of any clay depends, therefore, on (a) the evenness of the particle size, (b) the smallness of each particle size and (c) the degree of penetration of pore water into the clay and of its efficiency as a lubricating agent.

The plasticity, or lack of it, in any clay is of further significance in that it is directly related to two other important characteristics: porosity and shrinkage.

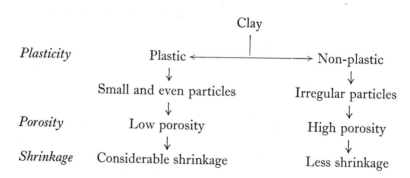

REACTION TO FIRE   A degree of plasticity is one of the features of unfired clay, the particles held together by their natural overlapping structure in the presence of water. As the form dries, however, pore water evaporates and the clay first becomes stiff (referred to as 'leather hard') and then dry.

When completely dry, clay forms are brittle and have to be handled with care. (The more plastic the clay from which the form was made the stronger it will be at this stage.) This fragile material is converted into a durable and strong one by a process of firing. The application of heat to the ware in a kiln effects a sequence of changes in the nature of the clay. During the first 200°C rise in temperature any water that remained trapped within the pores of the clay is driven out. Besides this pore water, however, clay also contains water bonded chemically into the molecule, as can be seen from its formula; by about 700°C this water is released and the material undergoes an irreversible chemical change, becoming hard and rock-like. Beyond this point further heat will cause a degree of vitrification to take place.

VITRIFICATION   This is a process of progressive melt within a clay body giving rise to the formation of glass bonds – and on occasions an interlocking crystalline structure – between the clay particles.

In porcelain wares the process of vitrification affects all the body constituents and reaches the point where true fusion between body and glaze is possible. Stonewares on the other hand retain a percentage of their components in an unvitrified state. These elements are compacted into a dense and impervious condition by the melting of neighbouring particles of lower fusibility within the body.

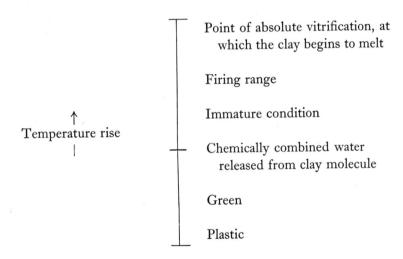

Temperature rise

Point of absolute vitrification, at which the clay begins to melt

Firing range

Immature condition

Chemically combined water released from clay molecule

Green

Plastic

The categories of ceramic ware based on their characteristic qualities

The work of studio potters in general can be divided into various categories, depending on such criteria as forming technique, firing technique, type of product, etc. One of the most fundamental factors, however, is determined by the temperature reached in the kiln during firing. Three clear divisions emerge, each with a characteristic chemistry of clay and glaze, known as earthenware, stoneware and porcelain. Of

these earthenware and stoneware are generally termed 'pottery' as distinct from the higher fired porcelain which is widely regarded as the aristocrat of the potter's art despite the fact that a high percentage of the recognized masterpieces of the ceramic arts are of pottery. It has been said that continental races (such as the Chinese and Europeans) have a natural predisposition towards porcelain while island people (such as the Japanese and British) find their best expression through the medium of pottery. Of course it is an easy exercise to think of numerous exceptions to such a broad generalization, but perhaps it contains a germ of truth and it certainly suggests interesting avenues of thought when we consider the ceramics of such countries as Korea.

EARTHENWARE   The majority of potteries that have been made during world history have been of the earthenware category. The common denominators are kiln temperatures below 1200°C and the use of common clays having a low maturation temperature due to their high content of active low temperature fluxes in which iron predominates. These clays, which normally fire to a red or brown colour, are found in most parts of the world and it is their availability together with the modest kiln temperatures required to fire them that accounts for a vast preponderance of earthenwares – of rich and various designs, styles and techniques – in all parts of the world. One thinks particularly of such brilliant achievements as those of China's Shang, Han and T'ang dynasties or the Japanese Jomon and Asuka wares, the elegantly decorated wares from Mesopotamia, the brilliant colour and flowing decorative arabesque of Islamic pottery, the sculptural forms of South America and the vigour of African and medieval English wares. This long tradition of earthenware, with its corollary of simple decorative devices and, if any, low temperature glazes, speaks eloquently of distinctive qualities of material, handling and appearance; of simple and direct processes and of great richness of creative possibility within a framework of functionality. These have led to a considerable renewal of interest in earthenware among contemporary studio potters.

STONEWARE   The type of pottery known as stoneware involves firing temperatures between about 1200 and 1300°C. As the name suggests the product is strong, durable, partly vitrified, dense and non-porous. Good natural stoneware clays, suitable for throwing without the necessity for some modification, are rare, but even those with certain deficiencies tend to be easily corrected and thereafter offer a clay of more satisfactory working qualities and fired appearance than is ever achieved from compositions of emasculated industrially prepared clays.

Historically, the temperatures necessary for the production of stoneware necessitated considerable advances in kiln design over the simple devices that sufficed for earthenware. The achievement of kiln temperatures of 1100°C+ in China circa 1100 B.C., for example, did much more than simply extend the capabilities of the contemporary potter; it opened up a radically new creative dimension that dominated the art until the isolation of kaolin enabled the T'ang potter to lay the foundations of the art of porcelain.

The great high temperature kilns of China and later Korea and eventually Japan involved more than a revolution in kiln design – more important, they led to a highly sophisticated understanding and control of fire itself. Even today there are in Japan kilns that have not changed substantially in design or firing technique over the last five centuries. These wood-devouring, smoke-belching monsters have a great personal presence and highly organic quality, reminiscent more of a great dragon hunched close to the earth demanding propitiation than a processing device for utensils.

All this seems to hold an important lesson for us. The digging of one's own local clay and preparation of our own necessities give us a deeper relationship and eventually some kind of intuitive rapport with our tools and materials when we come to use them; this, together with the deep and extended personal involvement that comes from designing and firing our own kiln, is perhaps the only way to set up that totally unified and organic situation out of which fine and artless pots are created. Historically, and particularly in the Far East, we can see that where and when this approach to the art of pottery persisted it invested the art with a creative strength that sustained it in vitality and virility, often over many generations.

PORCELAIN This is usually the product of 1300°C or more. (It is possible, in fact, by adjusting the formulations of body and glaze, to produce wares firing at approximately 1250°C which exhibit all the characteristics of porcelain.) Porcelain is totally vitrified and translucent, body and glaze are fully integrated and the ware is invested with an air of detachment and well mannered aristocratic elegance, to be appreciated, perhaps, cerebrally rather than sensually. The T'ing and Kwan Imperial wares of Sung China have a refined courtliness which, sadly, for all their artistic brilliance is somewhat alienating when compared to the involving qualities of stonewares such as the Chien Temmokus, the products of the Six Old Kilns of Japan or the Korean Ido bowls, all of which immediately establish an empathetic relationship through hands and sensitivities between ourselves and the nameless artisans who shared a love of sensuous clay, the lick of the loaded brush and the flush of pyromaniacal excitement in the stomach from a living kiln.

Types of clay

There are several different types of natural clay, which have been derived in their various forms as the result of the erosion of slightly differing parent rocks, of varying local conditions or of impurities they have gathered. All clay types, however, can be grouped into the two general categories of primary (or residual) and secondary (or transported) clays.

Primary clays are those which, having been created by erosion and chemical action, remain as a deposit on the site of their formation. Though usually irregular in particle size, primary clays tend to be chemically pure.

Secondary clays are those which have been transported by wind or water from their place of formation to be deposited elsewhere. Because of abrasion during transportation and additional interaction with eroding forces generally, the average size of secondary clay particles is reduced; also, their uniformity of size and shape is considerably improved. On the other hand, the transportation process may have introduced the clays to organic matter and mineral impurities (iron and coal are commonly-found impurities) – it is likely that the clay is a composite of a number of differing clay types which have been transported from various places of origin to be deposited together. Secondary clays are usually more plastic than primary clays.

Every clay has an intrinsic and individual character deriving from a combination of its physical type and chemical nature. Some clays dug directly from the earth are found to be suitable for making pots without any modification other than slaking and the normal processes of preparation. Other clays may be suitable only for certain specific ceramic techniques in their natural form, but may take on other possibilities after sieving or some degree of modification. Yet other clays may be useless except as a component in a calculated mixture of clays – called a clay body. Finally, some clays may contain such impurities as fragments of limestone which cause the shattering of wares in the kiln. The problems of removing such impurities are such that the clay is far better abandoned.

Clearly, if you are digging your clay from nature or buying from a commercial supplier you need to know the qualities and attributes of the individual clay types, both in the plastic and fired state, before you can use or combine them to their best advantage.

KAOLIN   The name Kaolin comes from the famous Chinese site, Kao-Lin, where this important type of clay is believed to have been first isolated. It is also commonly known as China clay.

In its best known form kaolin is a pure primary clay and is the nearest approximation we know to a pure clay and the mineral kaolinite. Because of its lack of impurity, it is white or near white in colour in the unfired state and pure white when fired. Most deposits (which can be found in

Cornwall, the U.S.A., particularly in the southern states, and continental Europe as well as in various parts of Asia) exhibit the typical qualities of primary clay in that they are irregular and large in particle size and, consequently, of poor plasticity. In this latter respect Florida kaolin is a notable exception, but it should be noted that this is a secondary rather than a primary deposit.

Kaolin is a highly refractory material, which is to say that it has a high resistance to heat with a melting point in excess of 1800°C. It forms the basis of porcelain clay bodies and of commercial white ware, but is used only as a component in pottery clay bodies to promote an extremely hard high fire capability.

Kaolin seldom comprises more than 20 per cent of the total bulk of a throwing stoneware body, although the percentage can rise to 30 for casting.

BALL CLAY Like kaolin, ball clay is derived from rock of the granite type and is of similar chemical composition. However, its increased exposure to decomposing forces and particularly to interaction with the chemical products of organic impurity have produced a clay which is a further step along the path of clay evolution from the plastic sedimentary kaolins such as are found in Florida. Despite their chemical similarity and their common ancestry the characteristic qualities of ball clay and kaolin as components in working clay bodies are almost totally opposite. As a result of its further evolution ball clay has achieved a remarkably small and even particle size and is therefore highly plastic. Like all extremely plastic clays, ball clay is excessively sticky in the slaked state and has a high degree of shrinkage; it is, therefore, unusable by itself for making pottery wares. It is, however, a valuable component in almost all contrived clay bodies for studio use, and particularly for throwing clays, to provide plasticity and assist in adding strength to the greenware.

Ball clay usually contains considerable quantities of organic impurity which colour the clay in its raw state – green and brown, and even black, are not uncommon. These colours burn away during firing to leave a product that is whitish, grey or pale buff in colour.

Ball clay normally contains small amounts of iron which act as a flux during firing and give it a lower maturation temperature than kaolin. Since the content of active flux is very small, however, ball clay remains a high temperature material requiring some 1300°C to tighten.

Up to 30 per cent of ball clay is commonly used in the formulation of clay bodies.

STONEWARE CLAY One of the basic materials of the studio potter is stoneware clay and natural deposits are often both highly attractive in fired appearance and usable for studio forming processes without the addition of other clays to modify their performance.

Stoneware clays are plastic secondary clays which fire to a white, grey or buff colour and have a maturation temperature in the range of 1200 to 1250°C, depending upon the content of fluxing impurities such as iron and feldspar.

FIRECLAY   The term 'fireclay' is used to describe an ability to withstand very high temperatures rather than a specific clay type. Fireclay is as commonly used to produce industrial refractories as it is by the studio potter.

Fireclays range from a coarse, non-plastic, granular form (used to open up clay bodies for slab and building techniques or for the promotion of thermal shock resistance) to comparatively fine grained and plastic varieties that are excellent in throwing clay bodies, where they contribute a distinctive and pleasing tactile quality.

EARTHENWARE CLAY   Functional earthenware is produced in most countries of the world, indicating the widespread occurrence of earthenware clay. It occurs at or near the surface and, due to the presence of considerable amounts of iron in one or other of its forms, may be brown, red, greenish-grey or tan in colour. It fires to a red-brown colour. Some deposits are smooth textured and of fine and even particle size. In such cases the clay tends to be excessively plastic and needs to be opened up before use with some non-plastic material (such as the appropriate grade of fireclay, sand or grog). Other deposits may be of the brick clay type containing much coarse sand which must be laboriously screened out if the clay is to be used for throwing; but the clay may be used in this extremely open form for larger building techniques, for Raku or for making bricks or saggars.

A reasonably fine earthenware clay can be expected to achieve its maximum density without bloating or distortion between 1000 and 1100°C. Even when fired to this maximum level, however, earthenware retains an absorption (porosity) level in the region of 10 per cent.

The prospecting and digging of clay; its testing and preparation for use

The most satisfactory, perhaps the only satisfactory, method of obtaining a working clay is to dig it directly from the earth and prepare it to suit your own needs. Clay can be found in most areas and, although the deposits may be unsuitable or far too small to justify any kind of industrial refinement, you will probably find that your local clay can be satisfactorily used, either by itself or with a little modification, for the production of wares of one type or another.

Before you even start to look for your clay, a visit to your local library, geological office or geography and geology department of your nearest college or university will almost certainly reward you with some precise information on where clay can be found near to the surface. They should also be able to furnish you with some valuable information concerning the clay type, its composition and likely impurities. If you are unable to acquire the information you need to enable you to pinpoint a potential clay bed the following procedure should be adopted:

Two types of map of the intended locality of dig must be obtained: the standard one inch to one mile topographical type and the geological survey map of the same area.

It must be remembered, of course, that geological structure is three dimensional and one of the main problems is to build up this three-dimensional image from the maps. The geological survey maps represent by line demarcation and colour code the geological features that outcrop at subsoil level. Since the private potter will not want to dig to great depths for his clay his first task is to establish on the geological map very general locations in which strata of possible interest come close to the surface. The topographical map now gives clues that help us to build up a mental picture of the geology of the area. Some varieties of rock tend to produce land forms of a distinctive type and many of these are clearly recognizable from contour patterns alone. In addition to this we can often gain further information from a brief consideration of local industry, place names (frequently very revealing), location of farms and vegetation types. Clay areas are relatively easy to recognize; the rock is easily eroded and outcrops can be expected to present a subdued relief at low altitudes. One tends to forget that clay is largely impermeable, a fact that is significant since it means that clay areas feature many small lakes and ponds in addition to a profusion of rivers and streams. Many clay areas have been cleared for arable use during the past centuries and a dense distribution of farms can also be a pointer to clay areas.

We now return to the geological map and find that the information acquired from the topographical map assists us in rejecting some possible areas and singling out others for further investigation.

The margins of the geological survey maps provide further data. Usually there are two columnar colour keys by which the map is interpreted. One represents superficial geological features; these areas tend to occur in small patches and their type is denoted by a code sign as well as a colour. Check this key to see if clay pockets are indicated and if they are not recorded this key may be henceforth ignored. If clay is indicated locate the occurrence on the map and add the location to your list of potential clay sites. The other key relates to the solid geology of the area. Sedimentary rocks are subdivided by formation and are colour coded. The hues relate to specific geological systems and also bear a letter coding (e.g., 'd' represents the carboniferous system). Igneous rocks are indicated separately from the sedimentary rocks and have a capital letter code. Within the sedimentary strata denoted in the key the oldest strata occur at the bottom of the column and the youngest at the top; it is worth noting that the clays under greatest compression tend to have become shaly and a simple generalization can be made that compression is usually directly proportionate to age. On some maps the depths of the strata are indicated visually in the key, in others numerically.

The geological map also has a section line across it and this section is projected as a topographical profile indicating the general relationship of the rock strata to the topography. With a little practice it is possible to visualize the section through any area on the topographical map from the information given in the geological version.

Thus by comparing the two maps it is usually possible to select one or two sites in the locality which seem to be potentially rewarding.

Again it is possible to save time through a little further library research. Each geological survey map sheet is accompanied by a volume of notes, called 'sheet memoirs', in which the findings of the survey together with pertinent observations on the local features are recorded. The final chapter of the sheet memoir is normally devoted to economic geology. This contains information on the industrial usefulness of the local minerals, using terms with which we are familiar, such as ball clay, brick clay, Fuller's earth, etc.

Observation of the landscape itself provides further clues: secondary clays tend to occur on gently sloping or undulating land, above which areas of sand, sandstone or flint clays frequently rise. (These sand/sandstone areas are often indicated by moorland type vegetation or coniferous woodland.)

In the final instance, of course, one has to investigate the site itself and take earth samples. Generally the clay will be covered with a layer of soil and, since clay seams can undulate, this may vary considerably in depth. Pits, local diggings, river valleys or railway cuttings may expose the clay and it can then be dug directly and easily. If the ground is uncut, however, it is necessary to make pilot bores to discover a point where the soil is shallow. A simple but efficient probe suitable for this work is illustrated.

Test any clays brought up from the bore before proceeding to a major digging operation.

N.B. Primary clays, like China clay, usually occur as pockets in granite areas and some of their closer relatives are also frequently found in locations in which granite predominates.

The chances are that you will find a common, red-firing secondary clay suitable for earthenwares. It can be recognized first by its colour, which will probably be red, light to medium brown or tan, but such a clay strata could also be grey, white, off-white or light green.

When handled raw clay has distinctive characteristics. If the clay is

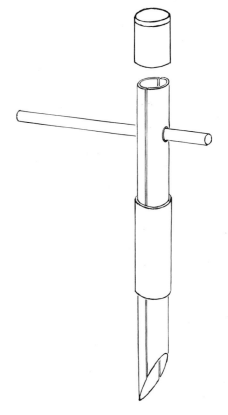

A simple probe for taking trial bores in search of clay located near the surface, consisting of a hard steel split tube (about 2 in., 50 mm, or more internal diameter), one or several sliding retaining sleeves – which remain above the surface – a heavy-weight cap and removable cross bar.
Sink the probe by hammering the cap; remove it by hammering upwards on the cross bar. Once removed from the ground the probe can be opened and a sectional plug of sub-soil examined.

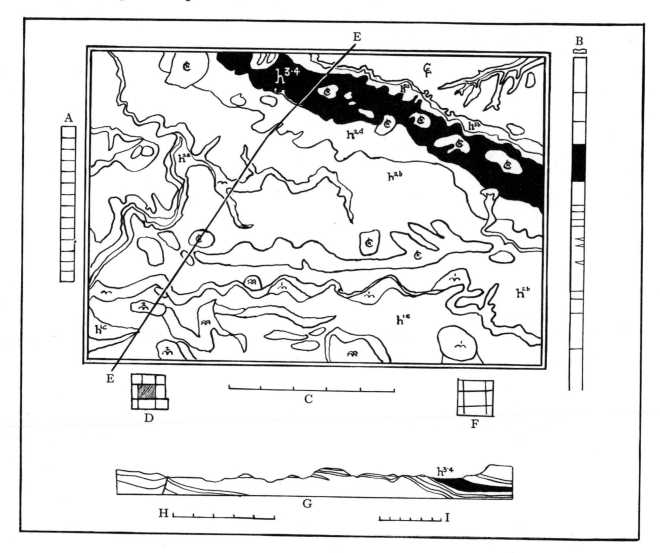

The Geological Survey Map. The written notes relating to the map indicate which strata are likely to provide workable clays. In this hypothetical case the notes suggest that a dig from a deposit of gault is likely to be the most productive. The symbol for gault is to be found in the key to the solid geology, B, and from this the areas of the landscape where the gault surfaces can be easily established on the main map. A study of this same landscape on a regular topographical map will disclose additional features which assist in pinpointing suitable areas for more detailed investigation and trial probes.

A   key to drift
B   key to solid geology
C   scale for main map
D   reference numbers of adjoining maps in same series
E–E line of section across map
F   reference numbers of maps in alternative scale
G   section through map along engraved line
H   horizontal scale of section
I   vertical scale of section

wet it can be expected to be slick on the surface and sticky. If dry, a deposit of plastic clay frequently exhibits cracks and pieces crumble loosely when crushed in the hands (particularly those with a high sand content).

Clear evidence of a rain water erosion can be seen on the surface of exposed clay seams, which contrasts with the more resilient appearance of rock strata.

If a deposit has an appearance which suggests that it might be a usable clay a simple test for plasticity should be carried out. If the clay is damp enough to be malleable knead a piece in the hands until fairly homogenous and roll it out until it is about the thickness of a pencil. If this can be bent around one of your fingers and the overlap squeezed together to form a ring which is not unduly cracked around its perimeter then the material can safely be taken to be a clay of good plasticity. A more sandy clay will, of course, crack a good deal more, but it may still be usable.

If the clay sample is dry, damp it down thoroughly with water and knead it in the hands. A plastic clay produces a rather shiny, glutinous and sticky mixture. The presence of an acceptable amount of sand makes the sample feel gritty, but the same general qualities, to a lesser degree, are present. After kneading, the sticky matter should be spread on to a wood or plaster bat to stiffen somewhat; it can then be re-kneaded and given the simple test for plasticity mentioned above.

Any clay which yields positive results to the above on-site prospecting tests deserves to be given a more thorough testing back at the studio to determine its exact character and usefulness and a sample of at least 5 lb (2 kg) dry weight should be lifted and carried back. The clay sample should be broken up into pieces and allowed to dry thoroughly.

SIMPLE STUDIO TESTS ON CLAY AND THE EVALUATION OF RESULTS

Limestone   Take a lump of the now dry clay, wrap it in a clean cloth and reduce it to a powder with a hammer. Three-quarters fill a standard chemistry beaker with diluted hydrochloric acid and sprinkle in the powdered clay sample. If, after the initial rise of air bubbles, bubbles of gas continue to rise to the surface of the acid or can be seen forming on the surface of the clay this indicates the presence of a considerable amount of lime. Such a clay sample is best abandoned, since it is generally easier to find an alternative source of workable clay than it is to remove the lime.

Soluble alkalis   The presence of soluble alkalis makes clay impractical. Their presence can often be recognized by a white staining on the surface of the dry clay. This can be seen in the on-site raw clay deposit but a similar staining or unsightly surface deposit may be demonstrated in the studio by drying out a sample of the contaminated clay from a slurry.

Shrinkage   The plasticity of a clay is directly proportional to the amount of water required to make a malleable material from the dry powdered clay. Excessively plastic clays are not only difficult to work but they are also subject to considerable shrinkage. This places considerable strain on the clay form during drying (particularly if drying is uneven) and also during firing. Handles, spouts and other applied parts are particularly vulnerable. Thus it is valuable to calculate the percentage of water of plasticity in any given clay, but even if you do not go to such lengths in testing your clay you should at least test it for shrinkage.

(a) Take a sample of the malleable clay and wedge it till homogenous. (b) With a rolling pin roll out the clay into an even slab of about $\frac{3}{8}$ in. (10 mm) thick. (c) Cut three rectangular tiles from the slab, each approximately 5 × 2 in. (125 × 50 mm). (d) Mark each tile with some identifying symbol in one corner; using the back of a potter's knife and a rule, score a fine line across the long face of each tile; with two marks that cross the first, mark off a length of precisely 100 mm (inches are impractical). (e) Allow the tiles to air dry, turning them over at regular intervals to prevent warping, which would make accurate measurement difficult. (f) When completely dry measure the section of the line which was formerly 100 mm. and calculate the shrinkage per cent as follows:

> Subtract the length of the line on the dry tile (in millimetres) from 100 mm. The remainder is the dry shrinkage of the clay as a percentage. Example for a clay that was found to shrink 6 mm. in drying: 100 mm − 94 mm = 6 per cent shrinkage.

Dry shrinkage percentages are generally between 4 and 15 per cent, with a low percentage being preferable for wares likely to suffer from drying strains. If the clay has a high shrinkage percentage it should be lowered by wedging in grog until a dry shrinkage retest gives a more satisfactory result without seriously impairing the workability of the clay. Use 80-mesh grog for throwing clay and coarser grades for building bodies, sculpture and Raku.

Fired shrinkage   Shrinkage continues during firing and normally results in a total shrinkage of between 12 and 15 per cent by maturation. Occasionally, fired shrinkage can be as high as 12 per cent, giving a total shrinkage as high as 25 per cent.

Shrinkage falls off with the approach of the maturation of the clay and for this reason each of the three test tiles is fired to predetermined increasing temperatures to establish the clay's development towards fusion. This information can be confirmed with a water absorption test on the fired tiles, but it is seldom necessary.

The following results were obtained from tests on a tan coloured clay dug from Suffolk, England:

PLASTICITY	Very plastic to sticky
LIME	None
SOLUBLE ALKALIS	None evident
ABOVE SAMPLE FIRED	Whitish deposit*
WATER OF PLASTICITY	31·5 per cent
DRY SHRINKAGE	8·9 per cent
FIRED SHRINKAGE AT SEGER CONE 04a	11·8 per cent with 5·8 per cent absorption
FIRED SHRINKAGE AT SEGER CONE 4a	12·0 per cent with nil absorption
FIRED SHRINKAGE AT SEGER CONE 8	Badly bloated and distorted

* The whitish deposit on the bisque ware was probably due to the presence of soluble sulphates in the clay. This condition is normally corrected by the inclusion of 1 – 2 per cent of barium carbonate in the body.

The material was therefore a low temperature, plastic earthenware clay. At 1020°C the absorption percentage was already low, indicating that the maturity of the clay was well advanced. When the temperature was increased substantially to 1160°C shrinkage was increased by only 0·2 per cent, but absorption of water dropped to nil, indicating that the material had reached its maximum degree of maturity before bloating, distortion and, later, melting.

The clay was eventually used in two forms:
1 unmodified with seger cone 05a Majolica type glaze
2 modified by the inclusion of 10 per cent kaolin, 5 per cent fireclay and 5 per cent flint and glazed at 1080°C.

Absorption percentage
   (a) Fire tile to predetermined temperature.
   (b) Weigh the fired test tile to nearest centigram.
   (c) Soak 24 hours in water.
   (d) Wipe tile dry.
   (e) Reweigh.
The percentage increase in weight indicates the degree of absorption of the clay under test at a given temperature.

Slip glaze   While testing an earthenware clay it is well worth testing it as a slip glaze, both by itself and with small additions of borax, feldspar or nepheline syenite.

When a clay has been sufficiently tested for its usefulness to be established a batch has to be dug from source. Since the preparation of clay for use is a rather laborious and protracted affair a sizeable amount should be taken in order to provide a really worthwhile batch of clay for your efforts.

If you are digging down from the surface, clear away all vegetation and surface soil and remove it some distance away so that it cannot fall down into the exposed clay during digging. Once the clay is reached, cut away the surface layer, leaving the clean seam exposed. Use a small sharp spade and be careful to take material only from the seam itself so as not to pollute it with matter from neighbouring strata. This is not easy, as seams of clay are often shallow and deposited at an angle to the surface.

CLAY PREPARATION The first stage in preparing the newly dug clay for use is to allow it to dry. Large lumps may be broken down with a hammer and the whole mass left out of doors to dry in the sun and wind. Most potters prefer to keep their clay under an open-sided but roofed structure.

When the clay is quite dry it is then thoroughly slaked with water (dry clay slakes much more easily and quickly than damp clay). Sprinkle the dry clay into rain water in barrel A and allow it one or two days to become totally saturated. The contents of the barrel should then be mixed up into a slurry with a wooden paddle. This should be repeated once or twice a day until most of the lumps have dispersed. It is important that plenty of water is used at this stage so that mixing produces a slurry of sievable consistency.

Place a 30-mesh sieve, supported on two wooden slats, over barrel B and ladle the slurry from barrel A through it. Still stiff lumps of clay may be returned to the slaking barrel while the humus, fine gravel and coarse sand that collects in the sieve, should be thrown away.

Each morning siphon the layer of clear water which will have appeared in barrel B back into barrel A (N.B. changing the water has a detrimental effect on plasticity), and remix the contents with the paddle. When eventually all the slurry, now in the form of a reasonably homogenous slip, has been transferred to barrel B a decision has to be taken as to the required texture of the eventual plastic clay. If a reasonably open pored clay is required allow the slip to settle overnight, siphon off the surplus water and thoroughly mix the remaining contents of the barrel. If any other clays are to be added to modify the working properties of the basic clay, they should be added in the form of slip, before this mixing. As soon as an even dispersal of the contents has been achieved remove the bung from the barrel and allow the slip to flow out into the drying bats.

If a fine grained clay is required, however, a different procedure should be followed. When all the slip from the slaking barrel A has been passed through the 30-mesh sieve into barrel B, additions of other clays

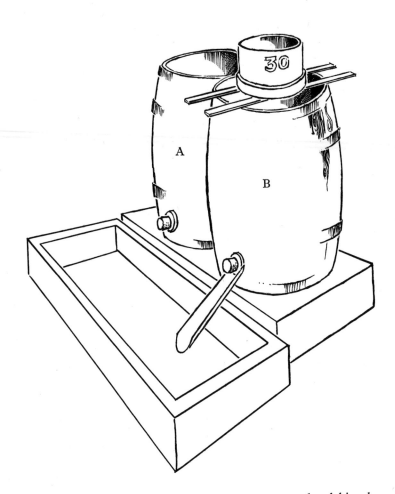

should be blended in, again in slip form. Clean out the slaking barrel A and place a 60-mesh sieve over it in the manner described above. The contents of barrel B should not be allowed to settle but should be passed immediately through the sieve back into barrel A. All the sand and large grained particles caught by the sieve should be discarded.

When the entire contents have been sieved a second time allow the material to settle overnight, siphon off excess water, mix the remaining slip and allow it to run out into drying bats.

Drying may be accomplished in bats or in troughs made of porous plaster or of fired fireclay slabs cemented together and supported by wooden or Dexion frames. These should be covered to keep out dirt and foreign matter. A rim of dry clay tends to form around the edge of the surface of the slip, which can easily result in an uneven consistency in the final clay. Each day this rim of stiffer clay should be pushed back into the liquid. The slip should stiffen in a few days to a point where it is sufficiently hard to have a preliminary kneading.

Opposite Japanese Tokoname ware. Height approx. 24 in. (609 mm). Michael Dean Collection, London. Photo: Derrick Witty

Kneading is best accomplished by the two-stage Japanese hand-kneading method. Divide the clay into lumps of approximately 15 lb (7 kilos) weight. Working on either a heavy plaster slab or firm wooden table, knead the clay – first by the *aramomi* (press) method, followed by the screw method known as *nejimomi*. When kneading clay it is important to remember that the weight of the upper torso and shoulders do most of the work; consequently the wedging board or table should not be so high that this weight cannot be effectively used; kneading is essentially a process of rhythm and coordination and seems to require undue strength and effort only until the technique is mastered.

Beat the mass of clay into a ball and place it in front of you on the wedging board. Place one hand on each side of the clay so that the palms of the hands are facing each other. Keeping the arms still, drop the hands from the wrist so that the fingers come near to the wedging board and the heels of the hands rest high upon the clay in a position where they can exert pressure coming from the shoulder. Straighten the hands at the wrist at the same time as pushing through the near one-third of the mass with all the weight of the shoulders. Repeat this process a few times until the typical shape emerges. The purpose of the *aramomi* kneading process is to compress the clay into a compact mass and to homogenize it by dispersing pockets of soft or stiff clay.

The *nejimomi* kneading which follows is designed to move the clay from the centre of the mass to the outer surface and back again to the centre. During this process final homogeneity is accomplished, any bubbles of air in the clay are brought to the surface and, perhaps most important of all, the lamellar particles are aligned in a structure conducive to maximum efficiency for throwing and other forming processes.

Beat the clay into an ovoid and place it before you on the wedging board at a diagonal to the plane of your body, closer to you on the left side and further away on the right. Place the left hand on the left centre of the clay and the right hand, again with fingers dropped from the wrist, on the apex of the mass. Straighten the right wrist while simultaneously pushing through the clay with both hands. The left hand turns and controls the direction of the clay while the majority of the body weight is channelled through the heel of the right hand. With repetition this movement sets up a spiral action within the mass and a hundred such movements are sufficient to achieve homogeneity.

Prepared clay should be stored in the individually kneaded masses and should be kneaded again before being used.

A galvanized metal or plastic dustbin makes a convenient storage container. Place a large water-saturated plaster bat in the bottom of the bin and cover with a wooden board. Stack the kneaded lumps of clay on the board and cover with damp cloths or sacking. Some potters include some lumps of aged soured clay among the new since this seems to

promote a more rapid bacterial action in the clay. (Sacking that has previously been used to cover aged clay can also be used to achieve the same ends, but care has to be taken that it is not left with the clay till it rots and sheds troublesome fibres on to the carefully prepared material.)

Blending a clay body from industrially prepared materials

Earthenware as a medium is underrated today, when sophisticated materials, equipment and fuels have brought high temperature wares within the capabilities of most of us. Yet the discipline of working close to nature, of being self-sufficient in terms of materials and firing while retaining a mindful respect for tradition and good craftsmanship is difficult to better as an experience. Simplicity, naturalness and directness are the products of such activity, and if one does not learn honesty and integrity from a close communion with the earth what hope is there of discovering them elsewhere? Certainly it affords us the opportunity to achieve an intimacy with each aspect of our work and, through deepening our personal involvement, extends our sensitivities. It remains only to express regret that too few students and potters reject the good clay under their feet for sterile and featureless industrial offerings, as well as missing the enriching and refreshing experience of getting back to fundamentals. Indeed, on a more mundane level, it can even be economically viable; while, if one should feel that 'individual character' is an indispensable prerequisite of clay, who in good conscience can afford the industrial product?

The majority of practitioners, however, cannot be expected to persist with the laborious processes or experience constant self-regeneration through working solely with local products. Many will want to prepare working materials from refined products, either in search of consistency of performance or to suit the specific needs and requirements of a particular process.

A clay body is a calculated combination of a number of various clays and other ceramic materials, in which each of the components is selected to contribute a necessary characteristic to the mixture as a whole. Clay bodies are usually not difficult to formulate and are simple to compound for use. There are three basic principles:

1 Get to know your raw materials and their characteristics. The variety that exists within types of kaolin has been mentioned and similar ranges of working qualities can be found within ball clays, fireclays, etc. Testing and experience provide the only real basis for knowing both the main and subsidiary qualities that make possible the selection of an appropriate variety of clay in any particular body.

2 Remember that simple solutions tend to work best. Do not use a combination of materials when a single alternative will do equally well.

Opposite Stoneware box by Ian Godfrey. Thrown form with sprigged high relief. Diameter 14 in. (355 mm). Photo: P. Macdonald

When in doubt it is best to follow natural compositions, structures and patterns of behaviour rather than seek out artificial solutions, however brilliant.

3 Maintain a respect for your material and your craft by not resorting to the common stratagem of faked appearances – such as that of simulating a 'natural' clay in a blended industrial composition. It is hardly worth the erosion of artistic integrity when natural appearance is so freely available.

BODY COMPONENTS

Saggar clay   This is similar to plastic fireclay and is used for the production of the refractory clay boxes in which wares may be placed during firing to protect them from the effects of direct flame. Its high maturation temperature coupled with plasticity and agreeable texture make it a valuable component in a stoneware body.

Grog   One of the most useful of ceramic body components, grog consists of a refractory clay which has been fired and then pulverized into granular form. Since grog is a pre-fired component its shrinkage has already taken place before use and it therefore serves to reduce the overall percentage of shrinkage of any body in which it is included. Additionally, the coarse granular nature of grog can be used to open up a dense clay body. It breaks up the lamellar alignments of constituent particles and can consequently be used to correct excessive plasticity. The same coarse form of grog serves to create passages through the material which assist in the evaporation of the pore water during drying and the escape of the chemically combined water which is released from the clay molecule during firing.

Below The *aramomi* (press) method of kneading clay.

Right The *nejimomi* (screw) method of kneading clay.

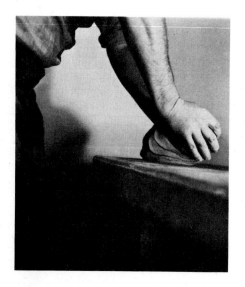

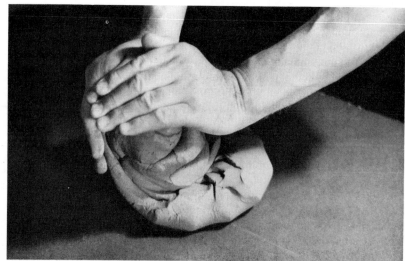

The reasons for the addition of grog to a clay body may be summarized as follows:

To reduce shrinkage
To increase porosity and reduce plasticity
(N.B. Grog of a mesh size between 80 and 120 is most effective in
reducing plasticity in throwing clays)
To reduce drying and firing strains
To reduce expansion and contraction stresses
To increase the general tolerance of the body to thermal shock in
Raku wares
To reduce slumping and facilitate the production of large forms
To add tooth and texture to the clay

Grog is classified by its granular size, that is, by the fineness of the
sieve mesh through which it can be passed. Grogs which have a mesh
size of between 80 and 40 are generally considered to be of medium
coarseness while sizes smaller than 80 mesh are fine. These two ranges of
grades are frequently used in clay bodies intended for throwing. The 40
to 20 mesh is rated as coarse grog and is used in bodies destined for
large scale work, slab building and sculpture. Very coarse grades of
grog (i.e., 20 to 10 mesh) may be included in clay to be used for sculptural
work in which coarseness of material is to be exploited as a feature.

Molochite   This is a special kind of grog. Whereas most varieties of
grog are pulverized either from fired fireclays or from brick, molochite
is produced from pure China clay. It is pure white in colour and extremely refractory, having a P.C.E. in excess of 1770°C. It tends to be
rather costly in comparison with the more common types of grog, but it
is invaluable when a purity of whiteness in the fired state is an important
factor in the design of the clay body.

Sand   This is an attractive material because it is natural, cheap and
easy to obtain. Its normal use is as a substitute for all or part of the grog
content. Fine white sand is frequently used as an additive to both
earthenware and stoneware bodies intended for throwing while the
more impure forms of sand, frequently polluted with iron, are commonly
compounded into modelling and building clays and coarse open bodies
such as Raku clay. Sand may also be added to a clay body for the
chemical reason of introducing silica to prevent crazing (see page 139).

Cornish stone, feldspar, nepheline syenite, talc, whiting, chalk and limestone
These materials are the most important of the body fluxes. They are the
prime agents in facilitating the melt of the clay and are consequently
largely responsible, directly or indirectly, for the strength, rigidity and
'ring' of the fired wares. The percentage of flux used in clay bodies is

To combine two masses of plastic clay, slice both masses with a potter's wire and intersperse them. Wedge them thoroughly by the *aramomi* and *nejimomi* methods until homogenous. Check by cutting through with a wire: the marbled pattern is typical of insufficiently combined clays.

usually small, but critical if exact qualities are to be obtained. Talc is particularly favoured as a flux for earthenware temperatures.

Bentonite   This is the most effective plasticizer per unit weight of any of the pottery components. It is a derivative of volcanic ash and has a remarkably fine and even particle size.

It is important that additions of bentonite are made to the clay body and thoroughly dispersed through it while the body is still in a dry powder form before slaking, since bentonite alone becomes unusably sticky when mixed with water. In the uncommon circumstances of needing to make an addition of bentonite to a plastic mass it is advisable to disperse the bentonite into some other suitable dry clay, slake this mixture and combine it with the basic plastic material by thoroughly kneading the two together.

Flint   This is one of the common forms of silica used in ceramics. Flint is an important filler in clay bodies, where it helps to regulate the melt as well as providing strength to the fired material.

Although flint may constitute up to 20 per cent of the total body bulk its amount must be carefully regulated in relation to the other body components since free silica causes dunting in the firing due to the expansions and contractions of what is known as 'quartz inversion'. Quartz inversion is a phenomenon which occurs in any of the forms of silica, such as flint. At normal temperatures quartz exists as an α form. When heated to 573°C it converts to a β form accompanied by a small but sudden expansion of 2·2 per cent. Free quartz undergoes a further conversion at 870°C together with a rapid expansion of 15 per cent. This whole process is reversible on cooling – to the accompaniment of contractions of similar degrees and suddenness. These changes of volume set up severe strains and tensions within the clay body and can result in the dunting mentioned above.

STONEWARE BODIES   The majority of clay bodies that are formulated in the studio are designed for use in the higher temperature ranges of stoneware and porcelain. The potteries known as stoneware derive their name from their hard and stone-like qualities as compared to those of earthenware. Their basic constituent is, in theory at least, stoneware clay. Natural stoneware clays are usually of sedimentary formation and found as one component within complexes of more refractory clays such as those of the fireclay family. Although deposits are to be found in most parts of the world they do not occur with the frequency of the earthenware varieties and, since the material has less industrial application than kaolin, for example, it is less widely available.

Stoneware clay may be defined as one which reaches a reasonable degree of maturity at 1200°C. It normally contains some impurities of iron, but not enough to flux it to a high density at low temperature. It fires to a grey, buff or tan colour and, in exceptional cases, to darker browns.

It is rare to find a stoneware clay which by itself satisfies all the requirements made of it. For this reason most working stoneware clays are bodies based on a given bulk clay. However, each stoneware clay that becomes available should be tested for shrinkage, porosity, plasticity and detrimental impurities and its properties compared with the desirable characteristics of a stoneware body, which are:

Maturation in the range 1200–1300°C
Freedom from distortion and cracking during drying
Total shrinkage of 12 per cent or less
Porosity between 1 and 5 per cent at maturity
Good plasticity
Some texture and content of non-plastics to support forms against slumping
Satisfactory colour
Low levels of soluble alkalis and organic pollutants

The characteristics of natural stoneware clays vary widely, particularly their maturation temperature/porosity relationship and their degrees of plasticity.

Stoneware with inlaid basalt by Tony Franks. Unglazed. Height 8 and 10 in. (200 and 250 mm).

The development of a satisfactory stoneware body is more a matter of progressive modification of the characteristics of an existing stoneware clay by adding other materials on an empirical basis than the application of a systematic theory of composition. For this reason careful testing of the basic stoneware clay that is to form the bulk of the body is important.

The process of determining what modifications are to be made is in itself difficult to define since it depends so much on the basic characteristics of the bulk clay. But the fundamental relationship towards which we have to work is a satisfactory reaction to fire in combination with workability. Let us say, for example, that the bulk stoneware clay is of a type that is coarse, non-plastic and excessively refractory and porous. Such a clay can be expected to have a low degree of shrinkage and in this respect can be reasonably expected to accommodate the considerable additions of plasticizing clay that are necessary together with a fluxing agent to lower the maturation temperature.

The following principles govern modifications to the most common types of stoneware clay:

Type A *Coarse, refractory, non-plastic:* modify with plasticizer and flux, either ball clay and feldspar or ball clay and red clay if colour is also required.

Type B *Excessively plastic, high shrinkage:* modify with non-plastic clay and filler, e.g. kaolin and grog.

Type C *Soft and crumbly when fired:* modify with flux, e.g. feldspar (or red clay if the stoneware clay can use additional plasticity).

Type D *Excessively dense when fired:* modify with more refractory materials such as fireclay and/or kaolin.

Type E *Larger forms slump or fired forms warp:* introduce fireclay, grog or kaolin.

Type F *Unsatisfactory colour:* to darken, introduce oxide or iron bearing clay; to lighten, substitute light burning materials.

The following percentages represent the largest amounts of constituent materials that are introduced into stoneware clay bodies, either for modifying an existing clay or in the process of formulation.

		per cent
BULK CLAYS	Stoneware	up to 100
	Fireclay (plastic)	70
	Fireclay (non-plastic)	30
	Saggar clay	70
	Kaolin	30
PLASTICIZERS	Ball clay	50
	Bentonite	3
	Red clay (maturation at 1100°C)	20
	Earthenware clay (maturation at 1000°C)	10
FLUXES (typical examples)	Feldspar	20
	Nepheline syenite	10
	Earthenware clay	10
	Talc	10
	Volcanic ash	10
FILLERS	Flint	20
	Grog	30
	Molochite	30
	Sillimanite	30
COLOURANTS	Earthenware clay	10
	Oxides – Iron	2
	Ilmenite	2
	Manganese dioxide	2
	Iron chromate	2

Suggested guidelines for stoneware bodies The following are suggestions only, since they depend on characteristics of individual materials, many of which you will be able to obtain in your local areas. These need testing and the remaining ingredients should be chosen for their compensatory qualities. Though you may expect your own composition to vary somewhat from those below, they may be useful as a basic guide.

Throwing bodies	Material	Contribution	Amount (per cent)
A (1250°C)	Stoneware clay	Basic clay	55
	Ball clay	Plasticizer	20
	Nepheline syenite	Flux	10
	Flint	Filler	10
	Earthenware clay (approx. 1050°C maturation)	Plasticizer Colourant Flux	5
B (1250 to 1300°C)	Stoneware clay		70
	Ball clay		15
	Grog (60 to 80 mesh)		5
	Feldspar		10
C (1250 to 1300°C)	Local stoneware clay (depending on its properties)		45–60
	Ball clay (indirectly proportional to plasticity of the stoneware clay)		20–30
	Flint		10
	60 to 80 mesh grog (if necessary to give body to the stoneware clay)		0–5
	Feldspar		8–12

Body for general use where no stoneware clay is available

1250 to 1300°C	Fireclay	40
	Kaolin	5
	Ball clay	35
	Flint	5
	Earthenware clay (low maturation 1050°C)	15

Body for building and sculpture

1250 to 1300°C	Fireclay	30
	Stoneware clay	10
	Ball clay	25
	Flint	5
	40 mesh grog	15
	Nepheline syenite	10
	Earthenware clay (low maturation 1050°C)	5

As a general rule 30 to 35 units by weight of water is necessary for each 100 units of dry clay, but this depends upon the average particle size. (The water content increases as the average particle size diminishes.)

LOW TEMPERATURE EARTHENWARE BODIES (UP TO 1100°C) The formulation of earthenware clay bodies from commercially prepared ingredients as a source of low temperature material provides an alternative to the laborious process of digging from nature. These formulated bodies are usually based on one of the commercial red clay powders available from ceramics suppliers. Tests on such a clay may show it to be very plastic and have a low maturation temperature (around 1000°C) while others are more granular in texture, less plastic and comparatively refractory. There are, of course, other varieties of red clay with characteristics between these two extremes.

These basic clays can form a workable body by modifying them as follows.

Fusible, over-plastic basic clay is modified with refractory materials such as kaolin, fireclay, flint or grog. These raise the maturation temperature, open up the pores of the clay to improve drying, reduce plasticity and impart a more pleasant 'feel' to the smooth basic clay. If a stoneware clay is available a percentage of it may be mixed with the earthenware clay which, with the addition of grog, may be a simple method of achieving more satisfactory test results. In all cases the basic clay can be expected to comprise at least half the final body.

Granular, relatively refractory and non-plastic clay requires modification in two ways. First, the plasticity must be improved by adding up to 40 per cent of ball clay (although the usual addition seldom exceeds one quarter of the final bulk). If a large percentage of ball clay seems to be necessary to achieve reasonable plasticity, 2 or 3 per cent of bentonite may be used since it is several times more efficient a plasticizer per unit weight than ball clay.

The second modification necessary is to lower the maturation temperature of the clay. This is accomplished by combining an active flux into the formula. Feldspar, the most frequently used body flux in higher temperature bodies, is ineffectual in the low earthenware temperature range. The most practical alternative is nepheline syenite, which is a relative of feldspar but has a lower activity threshold. The maximum addition of this material is 25 per cent. Talc or iron oxide are alternative simple fluxes. Talc is effective when combined with another flux as a supplement, but it is comparatively weak by itself and therefore has to be used in large quantities if a considerable degree of fluxing is necessary. Since talc has a negative effect on plasticity its usefulness as a flux is questionable and it is probably best restricted to the special cases of producing white firing earthenwares or casting clays. Iron oxide is a very effective flux, particularly when a dark colour is desirable and another flux is also present. The usual maximum inclusion is 6 to 8 per cent.

Frits are compounds of materials which, for various reasons (such as the solubility of some of the components in their natural state or the toxicity of others) have been mixed together and heated in a crucible until they have melted and fused together. This compound is shattered and reduced back into a powder in a ball mill, ready for inclusion in ceramic formulations. In the fritted form the soluble or toxic components are converted into a compound which, although retaining the potential chemical effectiveness of its components, renders them stable and non-poisonous. Frits are therefore able to harness the highly effective fluxing qualities of soluble materials such as borax and such toxic ones as lead. The two common types of frit are those used to flux glazes and clay bodies. Body frits tend to be less active than those employed in glaze formulation, but they are extremely effective for their purpose. Frits can comprise up to 25 per cent of a low temperature earthenware body, although it is not normally necessary to use even half this amount, especially when other fluxes are present.

Suggested guidelines for low temperature bodies	*per cent*
Red clay	20–80
Ball clay	0–40
Fireclay	0–25
Grog	0–15
Fritted body flux	0–25
Talc	0–20
Nepheline syenite	0–25
Iron oxide	0–8
Flint	0–10
Kaolin	0–20
Plastic kaolin	0–25
Stoneware clay	0–30
Bentonite	0–3

Examples
To make a good throwing body

Plastic, fusible red clay	55
Fireclay	10
Stoneware clay	15
Kaolin	5
Flint	10
Grog (fine grade)	5

To make a light burning body

Plastic kaolin	22
Ball clay	22
Stoneware	18
Fritted body flux	12
Nepheline syenite	12
Talc	6
Flint	8

To make a general purpose clay

Non-plastic, refractory red clay	55
Stoneware clay	10
Ball clay	25
Bentonite	2
Fritted body flux	3
Iron oxide	2
Nepheline syenite	3

MIDDLE TEMPERATURE RANGE RED WARES (1145 to 1190°C) Both low temperature earthenware and stoneware have their respective bodies of devotees as well as a few self-confessed fanatics and indeed one can understand the attractions of and the commitments to either. The negative feelings that each feels for the work of the other are also not hard to appreciate; the industrial sources of the materials often used by the stoneware potter, the feel of stoneware table wares against the lip or the sound when a knife scrapes across a stoneware plate all evoke a kind of revulsion in the sensibilities of the committed maker of earthenwares. On the other hand the maker of stonewares prefers the hardness of his product and the wider range of glazes readily available to him.

The mid-range wares, on the other hand, seem to enjoy less devotion and tend to be the object of little or no fanaticism. This is surprising, for they are much more than a compromise between the two popular classes of ware. Middle temperature wares share with stoneware qualities of fired strength and low porosity. The clays from which the wares are made have a good plasticity, pleasant feel and usually a medium to dark red-brown colour. The glazes that relate to the middle range wares have wide possibilities of surface and can retain the brilliant colour qualities of the low temperature earthenwares within a glaze that is durable and hard enough to resist wear. Other advantages are that the firing cycle is shortened somewhat and that the lower operating temperatures exact a less heavy toll on electric kiln elements, fire brick, kiln shelves and kiln furniture in general.

The mid-range is ideal for much school and college pottery. For the private potter also, all the above advantages apply together with a significant reduction in fuel costs.

Mid-range clay bodies are normally formulated and compounded rather than dug since clays which exhibit the right qualities of maturity and porosity at about 1150°C are comparatively rare. This is not to say that they do not exist but, unlike the fusible earthenware clays which can be found almost anywhere, you may have to accept that you will not be able to dig it locally. If such is the case one has either to buy the clay from a merchant or modify one which naturally fires at a higher or lower temperature.

Bodies should be designed to have a shrinkage not exceeding 12 per cent and a porosity of about 3 per cent.

Suggested limits for mid-range bodies	*per cent*
Earthenware clay or stoneware clay	10–50
Fireclay	0–25
Plastic kaolin	0–25
Ball clay	0–40
Grog	0–15
Bentonite	0–3
Flint	0–10
Nepheline syenite	0–25
Talc	0–15
Example	
Stoneware clay	22
Earthenware clay	10
Ball clay	20
Bentonite	2
Fireclay	20
Nepheline syenite	10
Flint	6
Grog (fine mesh for throwing)	10

COMPOUNDING THE PLASTIC BODY FROM THE DRY MATERIALS The design stage is the most important part of the production of a satisfactory clay body and it is essential that you know exactly the characteristics you want the body to possess before you start. This allows one to proceed by a fairly logical line of reasoning towards a formulation which will give a close approximation to these requirements. Small samples must then be fired and tested, after which further modifications will be made to correct minor defects in the design. Once a final design has been achieved, tested and proved to satisfy precise requirements a batch can be made up for use.

The size of the batch will, of course, depend upon a number of factors: the number of people for whom it is being made, their proficiency, the production process to be used (for example, throwing on the wheel can be expected to consume a good deal more clay in a unit of time than, say, slab building), how long the batch is to last and the degree of mechanization of your compounding facilities. Experience of course will soon provide an answer to the problem, but as a rough guide a reasonably competent student may throw more than 100 lb (45 kg) of plastic clay in a day's work, of which 35 per cent will be water.

Mixing a small batch by hand

1　Weigh out the dry materials. (If any contain lumps pass through a 20-mesh sieve.)
2　Mix the constituents together by hand in a suitable container.
3　Obtain a complete dispersal by passing the entire contents through the 20-mesh sieve twice, with a hand mixing between sievings.
4　Weigh water and pour into a non-ferrous container.
5　Sprinkle the clay mixture on to the surface of the water, cover and allow to slake for three or four days.
6　If necessary, dry out excess water by spreading the clay on a plaster bat for a few hours.
7　Knead the clay thoroughly.
8　Wrap in polythene and store away from extremes of temperature till required.

Larger batches of clay can be made up on the ground in a manner similar to that used to mix concrete. Place the dry ingredients on a flat surface and thoroughly intersperse them by mixing with a shovel; sprinkle on water and mix. This process is continued until the required plasticity is obtained. It should then be allowed to mature for a few days before being kneaded.

Mechanical clay mixers　Present-day commercial clays are generally highly refined and even air floated to ensure a fine and even size of powder; consequently the traditional methods of mixing the clay into a liquid slip before drying into a plastic mass may be unnecessary and one can proceed directly from powder to plastic state by using a mechanical clay mixer.

A number of ceramic supply companies now market machines for this purpose, which have a suitable capacity for the private pottery, college or art school department of ceramics. One popular design has rotating blades within a drum in the style of a baker's dough mixer.

The dry components of the clay body are weighed out and poured into the drum together with the measured weight of water. The drum is covered and the contents mixed by power from an electric motor. A plastic body can be produced in less than half an hour by this method. The clay does, however, need to be left for a few days to fully slake and mature before use.

Clay preparation by blunger and filter press　Homogenous dispersals of clay in water are known as slip. These are normally produced in a device known as a blunger, which consists of a pair of slow moving, mechanically driven paddles which agitate a mixture of water and clay within a drum. Blungers are particularly efficient for producing homogenous fluid slips from lumps of natural clay. The process normally takes several days. When all the lumps have been dispersed by the action of the blunger the slip is allowed to settle naturally, after which the excess of water may be syphoned off from the top, leaving the heavy slip below with possibly some heavy impurities gathered beneath it at the bottom of the drum.

The slip may be dried, as mentioned earlier, in drying troughs or by the action of a filter press. This mechanical device pumps heavy slip under considerable pressure into fabric filters, which allow the water to escape but which retain the clay in a much stiffened and plastic condition.

Clay storage and reconstitution

Whenever a fresh batch of clay has been compounded or achieved by any of the possible processes it is extremely beneficial to allow it to mature. The clay should be thoroughly kneaded and stored, in the presence of some old clay, within a bin or bunker lined with polythene sheeting. During this process of maturation plasticity improves due to the thorough penetration of water into all the pores of the clay and to the development of colloidal gels within the pore water as a result of bacterial activity.

The cost of acquiring a satisfactory working clay body may well be expensive, if not financially, perhaps in terms of effort and involvement. It is only natural, therefore, that wastage should be avoided where possible.

Any pottery produces scrap clay; also, a number of pieces are invariably rejected for one reason or another before firing and there are also those pieces which, unhappily, get broken. All this clay, provided that it has not been fired, can be reclaimed and reconstituted back into plastic clay for further use.

Pound the dry clay into small pieces and place in a plastic or galvanized bin. Sprinkle the pieces liberally with water, cover with damp sacking and seal the container. Turn the clay daily and sprinkle with more water until the fragments have absorbed enough to be kneaded back into a plastic state. Alternatively, the clay may be mixed and homogenized (and with some models also de-aired) by passing it through a pug mill which grinds, compresses and kneads the clay back into a smooth, compact and even consistency, ready for use.

Store as normal until required.

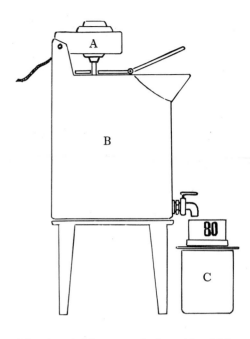

The electric blunger, a device with which clay powder, raw lump clay or clay for reconstitution is reduced to a slip. It consists of a container, B, which is fitted with a lid and often with a hopper, into which water and clay are deposited together. This mixture is agitated by a slowly rotating electrically driven paddle, A. The constant slow motion over a period of several days reduces the mixture to a reasonably homogenous fluid which is run off through the valve at the base of the blunger directly through a screen. The screened slip which collects in the container, C, may then be stiffened into a plastic working mass in a filter press or in drying bats.

Pottery Making: A Complete Guide

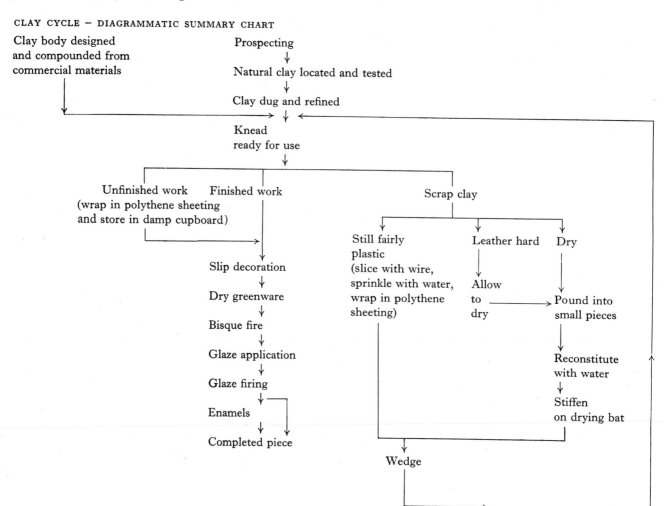

Clay body designed and compounded from commercial materials

Prospecting
↓
Natural clay located and tested
↓
Clay dug and refined
↓
Knead ready for use
↓

Unfinished work
(wrap in polythene sheeting and store in damp cupboard)

Finished work
↓
Slip decoration
↓
Dry greenware
↓
Bisque fire
↓
Glaze application
↓
Glaze firing
↓
Enamels
↓
Completed piece

Scrap clay

Still fairly plastic
(slice with wire, sprinkle with water, wrap in polythene sheeting)

Leather hard
↓
Allow to dry

Dry
↓
Pound into small pieces
↓
Reconstitute with water
↓
Stiffen on drying bat

Wedge

2 Ceramic design: principles and practicalities

Ultimately no aspect of pottery is more important than any other; it is the art of perfect order and harmony. To achieve excellence in it we must commit ourselves to a rigorous discipline of total honesty to our materials and develop the kind of creative integrity which will cause us to instinctively reject any act or process which debases our highest perceptions and the great traditions of the art we practise. The potter must strive to create a work which exudes an unequivocal sense of rightness, suitability and harmony between all its aspects. There should be no hierarchy – that is to say no element which overpowers the rest.

Harmony, however, cannot be achieved immediately and in learning about pottery one must accept principles which one will transcend when greater experience and insight is gained. In learning about pottery it is wise to accept the proposition that involvement with clay is the most important aspect of the art, having precedence over decoration, technique and even that most exalted of all aspects of pottery – glaze. Clay and the potter share a fundamental relationship upon which rests any achievement. The processes which follow the basic formation of the pot are, at best, a perfectly judged complement or, at worst, mere embellishment. Later, the basic pleasures of a handful of clay lead into the study of such seemingly diverse fields as chemistry, geology and structural mechanics and, indeed, may eventually bring the potter to the feet of the queen of the humanities – philosophy.

In an age split apart with miraculous technological advance and philosophical alienation pottery offers a real possibility of achieving meaningful personality enrichment and mind expansion through a commitment to, and involvement in, the primal elements of the universe, earth, air, fire and water. It is an art through which man works at re-establishing a harmony with nature (now virtually lost to society in general) and attuning his creative processes to natural processes, re-forging basic links between man and nature so that eventually he becomes a tranquil vehicle through which nature flows.

Many people are attracted to pottery by the directness of the experiences it offers, its empirical processes and lack of intellectual pose. The novice, however, fails to apprehend the depths hidden beneath tranquil and simple appearance, erroneously believing it to be easily achieved. The sculptor Brancusi, that great master of simple form, penetrated to the very heart of this problem when he observed

Family of jars fitted with sculptural stoppers, by Walter Keeler. Height 4½ in. (114 mm).

'simplicity is at bottom complexity and one must be weaned on its essence to understand its significance'.

The principles of ceramic design then are not matters of technique or concept, of scientific rationale or mechanics; they are more fundamental, more humanizing and much more difficult to realize and sustain. The practicalities of ceramic design all reflect these basic principles.

Form

Clay is used in many states and is worked by very many techniques. Leather-hard clay may be carved, plastic clay thrown, slabbed, coiled, pressed or moulded; in its liquid form of slip, clay is used for casting. The clay designed and produced for each process has certain qualities of plasticity, texture and surface, and the forming technique used also imparts specific characteristics to the emergent form. It is a basic dishonesty and design abomination to produce slip-cast wares, for example, that simulate the plastic qualities of throwing just as it is to use clay in any of its forms to ape the appearance of metal, glass, plastic or wood. The debasement of materials and the prostitution of visual appearances in our century springs largely from a lack of discrimination of the consuming public, but it has also been stimulated by the designer prepared to compromise the integrity of his craft.

One of the exciting qualities of pottery is that one can re-create in the hands and mind the experience of the forming process. Thus the sense of organic and vigorous growth, of the hand at work within and of the softness of the clay at the time of working are all qualities of thrown wares that should be evident, while the slow and asymmetric upward growth of the coil pot should create a product that not only exhibits different concerns on the part of the potter but also evokes a different reaction from the observer. The pot must speak to us of its genesis and unfold a chronicle of the 'process of becoming'.

Function

As well as aesthetic considerations there is also the matter of satisfactory functional performance and although often thought of as separate, the two aspects are inseparable. Pots intended for use must perform that function easily and without inconvenience to the user. The spout or lip which will not pour well, the ill-placed handle, the insecure teapot lid or even the clay body which transmits so much heat that a coffee mug is unholdable are all guilty of basic functional faults which no aesthetic merit can erase. Frequently, design faults such as these are only gradually eradicated over a long period of repetition and production, which, incidentally, like the digging of clay, offers a chance to examine a problem in depth and, far from being tiresome or boring, is extremely stimulating and rewarding in terms of perception development.

Appearance

In addition to his sculptural involvement with the creation of the form itself the potter is in most cases responsible for its visual appearance in terms of decoration and glaze. It is difficult to generalize about the relationships that work well between form and these two elements. Vigorous brushwork can enliven a passive cast or moulded form (as Kenzan I often demonstrated); in other cases, such as the monochrome glazed Chinese wares of the T'ang and Sung dynasties, like harmonizes with like as a simple fluid glaze reflects the easy fluid throwing technique of the nameless potter. Yet again a form may be left undecorated if the potter feels that the tactile qualities of its surface are a sufficient complement to the shape.

In each case the important common factor is the potter's awareness of the needs of the piece. At its best pottery demonstrates total unity between concept and execution of form, decoration and glaze so that one feels the relationships to be virtually inevitable. The potter demonstrates that his creative intelligence is of an all-embracing type, which could be described as a diffuse focus. The form receives exactly those additions it needs, neither more nor less, which are executed with admirable restraint because, although they may not have been consciously preconceived, they were all along implicit in that synthetic state of awareness which is the hallmark of advanced performers in this most subtle of arts.

Of course, we cannot expect to achieve such high levels of performance easily or quickly but by recognizing and being aware of such advanced achievements and studying the traditions which bore them we can direct the path of our own development surely towards the highest standards.

3 The basic forming techniques

Pinching

The technique of pinching out bowls from a small ball of clay is one of the most ancient methods of forming pottery and dates back to prehistoric times. It is such a simple technique that many students consider it unworthy of attention – a mistake that many mature potters in Korea and medieval Japan did not make. The pinching method is very appealing and is ideal both as a training technique for acquiring the basic sensitivities to clay and for demonstrating the most advanced and subtle displays of manipulative skill.

Pinch formed pots have a character that is quite unique. Their scale is the scale of the hand and their form relates directly to the shapes of cupped hand and finger tips. In the walls of a pinch formed pot can be felt the potter's developing concerns as his ball of clay grew from potential to actuality – the evidence of an intimate relationship between maker and material.

To make pinch pots we must first select or prepare a suitable clay body. The essential characteristics are that it must be fine in average particle size and of excellent plasticity so that it will withstand the extrusion of the clay as it is squeezed thinner and thinner by the fingers. It must be capable of withstanding prolonged contact with the hands without drying out, losing its plasticity or cracking. At the same time it must have sufficient mechanical strength to support the thin walls typical of pinch pots during production and drying. Fine grained plastic earthenware clays containing about 15 per cent of the finest mesh sizes of grog are thus particularly suitable for the technique. The prepared clay should be moist without being sticky, and well kneaded.

Take a piece of the clay and roll it in the hands to form a ball slightly smaller than a tennis ball. It is important to smooth out any creases left in the surface of the ball after rolling. Make up only one ball of clay at a time and keep the rest of the batch wrapped in polythene sheeting so it retains the water content essential for malleability.

Holding the ball of clay in the cupped left hand, push the thumb of the right down through the centre of the ball till it is about $\frac{1}{2}$ in. (13 mm) from the far exterior surface. With the four fingers of the right hand held together on the outside of the ball and the thumb inside, now perform a gentle squeezing motion to thin the clay as the whole mass is turned constantly by the left hand. It is important that the motions

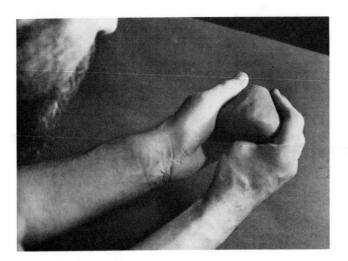

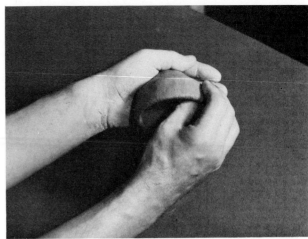

Left Opening up the centre of the ball of clay.

Right Modelling the upper part of the pinched form.

made by the fingers to thin the walls of the form do not attempt to reduce the thickness of the clay by too much in any one motion; the pinching should be light and even and the form should need to be turned and pinched through several full revolutions before a satisfactory thickness (usually about $\frac{1}{4}$ in. or 6 mm) is achieved at the base.

Now that the lowest reaches of the bowl have a provisional form, the modelling is continued progressively up the walls of the pot, working as before in a constant gentle circular motion. The left hand has the essential job of controlling the form of the bowl against its natural tendency to flare outwards as well as continuously turning the form. The mass of clay, as yet unmodelled, which will eventually form the upper reaches of the bowl's walls should be kept thick and compact, passing through the wide 'V' in the hand between thumb and fingers. If this mass is thinned out too early it will dry and crack when the lip and upper part of the walls come to be formed.

Once a good technique has been developed pinched bowls can be produced with well controlled profiles and complete absence of cracking during forming. Less practised potters, however, commonly encounter two problems: (a) the form slumps out of control and (b) the clay develops cracks in its surface or even splits. Slumping may be the result of too small a percentage of supporting material in the clay body, in which case the percentage content of fine grog should be increased. Alternatively, it may result from weak handling of the form by the left hand. A constant, firm and restraining pressure must be exerted against a natural tendency for the form to spread outside the limits which can be controlled by one hand. Do not attempt to rest the form on a table or working surface, as this quickly distorts the soft clay and robs the form of its particularly intimate relationship with the hands. Cracking is usually the result of the clay drying out too much during working and losing its plasticity; this is usually the result of poor technique, which causes the clay to be handled excessively during forming. If cracking does occur cover the pot with a damp cloth for a few minutes to allow moisture to be reabsorbed. The cracks may then be smoothed over with the finger tips.

The top of the walls and lip should be modelled with particular care. Pinch up the walls with extreme precaution and strengthen the lip by compressing it downwards slightly with pressure from the right index finger while carefully supporting the clay on each side with the thumb and second finger. Damp down the lip of the bowl with a moist sponge if cracks appear.

The profile of the lip of pinched bowls usually rises and falls in a gentle asymmetric curve; this is a natural product of the process and, although the lip may be cut flat with a blade after the clay has stiffened a little, this destroys one of the basic characteristics of the technique. It is far better to produce a prescribed form by practised technique than to falsify a form which is in any case emblematic of the forming processes involved. The compressed lip should be smoothed with slightly dampened finger tips and polished after a few hours of drying.

When the basic form of the bowl has been fashioned it is usually necessary to start again from the bottom, to pinch out minor inconsistencies of thickness.

Finally, a low foot may be raised from the slightly thicker clay always left at the base of pinched bowls. An alternative method of creating a foot on a pinched bowl is the coiled method (see page 49) after the form has stiffened somewhat. Score the surface of the bowl with a potter's pin where the ring of clay is to be added and work in a good application of slurry. Roll out a coil of clay of suitable dimensions and press it into position on the circle of now tacky slurry. Press down some of the clay forming the inner and outer circumferences of the coil and weld them thoroughly into the basic form of the bowl. The remainder of the coil may then be pinched up to form a footring.

For the same reason it is aesthetically undesirable to cut off the natural lip of the bowl it is also undesirable to scrape down the inner and outer surfaces to achieve a more symmetrical appearance. Of course it is possible to do so and the best time is when the clay is still damp and yet has stiffened to a leather-hard condition that allows the clay form to be handled without distortion. A scraper made from a kidney shaped piece of flexible metal or a piece of broken hack-saw blade are both suitable tools.

The basic form of the bowl once made may also be modified by beating it gently with a flat piece of wood (called a 'paddle').

Surface decoration may be added to the form if it is thought desirable, or motifs may be incised or pressed into the surface.

Once the bowl form has been mastered numerous other shapes may be produced. The pinching technique is useful for producing small covered boxes; bottles may be made by joining two pinched bowls lip to lip. The lips of two leather-hard bowls should be thoroughly scored with a potter's pin and an application of slurry worked into the surface of each. When this slurry has stiffened appreciably a second thick application should be made and the two bowls joined together immediately. Twist the two bowls against one another slightly to ensure thorough adhesion and smooth over the exterior join. Cut open the foot of the upper bowl to form a neck opening and, using a tool (a shafted bone with a prominent ball joint is ideal) inserted through this hole, smooth over the slurry which has been exuded during the luting process, making a good join inside as well as out. A neck may be modelled on the pinched bottle by the coiling process or a thrown neck may be added.

Elbow pots are a variation on the pinch pot technique and, although now almost extinct, the technique may be interesting as a discipline. The elbow pot was a common method used in Korea and Japan to form simple and unsophisticated bowls. The technique involved pressing and turning a small ball of clay with the left hand on to the right elbow, which acted as a conical former. Although the bowls were intended to be the contemporary version of present-day disposables some examples which remain demonstrate a vigorous style of modelling, thin walls and excellent control.

Like the pinched pot, the elbow pot demonstrates that skill, simplicity, naturalness and sensitivity are the main necessities in the pottery process and should not be thoughtlessly abandoned in favour of mechanical equipment and processes.

Coil building

The art of building pots from coils is so ancient that it is impossible to say when or where it began, but there exist fine refined Chinese examples dating from the thirteenth century B.C. and particularly dramatic and inventive Japanese pots dating from the Jomon period (*c.* 300 B.C.).

The process is delightfully simple and therefore allows a maximum of thought and involvement to be brought to bear on the growing form. No tools are really necessary to diffuse concentration (although use can be made of a coil cutter, potter's pin, sponge, a flexible metal scraper and other such standard tools).

The clay for coil building should contain about 10 to 15 per cent of mixed medium and fine grog and should be made up to a rather softer consistency than for the other basic processes. It must be thoroughly kneaded before use.

MAKING THE COILS   Cut up the basic mass of clay with a wire. Take one section of the clay at a time and roll it between the hands to form a thick solid cylinder. Place the cylinder on a wooden topped table and roll it backwards and forwards with the hands into a long uniform coil. Rather more skill is required to roll an even coil than might be imagined; it is important not to press too hard on the clay during rolling; make sure the coil performs a complete revolution during the rolling process (too short a roll produces oval coils). Roll with the full flat of the palm of the hand and fingers; keep the fingers together to avoid making ridges in the coil. As the coil gets longer it may crack from excessive torque at the point of transition between its static and moving parts. To eliminate this tendency, lift the clay free of the table with one hand immediately ahead of the rolling hand as it progresses along the coil. When a full length coil (usually $\frac{1}{2}$ to 1 in. or 12 to 25 mm thick) has been rolled it should be laid out between pieces of polythene sheeting or damp cloth while the next coil is prepared. Roll all the coils necessary to make the piece (or the lower passages of a large piece) before starting the construction.

Alternative methods of making coils are by extrusion from a wad box or by cutting coils from a thick slab of kneaded clay with a cutter. Square rather than round coils are sometimes used: a flat slab of clay is rolled out (with a rolling pin) to a uniform thickness on a length of cloth or sacking and cut with a potter's knife.

CONSTRUCTING THE BASIC FORM   To construct a coil-built form three basic components are needed: a flat clay base, the prepared coils and a little thick slurry made by mixing a little of the coiling clay with some water.

Roll a piece of the kneaded clay into a ball and smooth out any creases in it. Flatten the ball on the table to form an even disc of about the same thickness as the coils. This disc, which will form the base of the pot, may now be placed in the centre of a small round wooden or asbestos bat so that it will turn on the table to facilitate even working. Alternatively, it may be set on a bench banding wheel, which allows the growing form to be turned around as necessary during the forming process.

The first coil is joined to the top surface of the disc around its perimeter. The perimeter should be roughened with a potter's pin (or a finger nail) and a light application of slurry made to it. Place the coil on the base, ensuring that it is making good contact with the base at all points. Cut off excess coil length and join the two cut ends together, working the clay from the two pieces together so that all semblance of the join is eliminated. A strong bond between the coil and base can now be created by pushing down a little of the clay forming the inner circumference of the coil and welding it into the clay of the base.

The top surface of the attached coil is now thoroughly scored with the pin and slurry is applied to prepare it for the addition of the second coil.

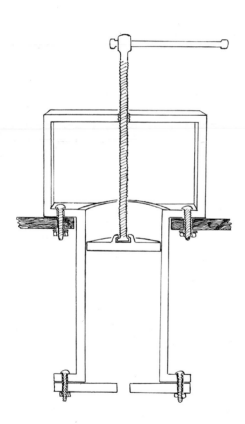

Wad box (or wad mill), a simple device for extruding coils. The size and shape of the coils can be varied by changing the pattern of the die plate.

At this point it is necessary to have some idea of the intended shape of the pot, since if the form is to belly out as it rises the second and subsequent coils must be joined slightly towards the outer edges of their predecessors. If the form of the pot is to be convergent they are each joined to the inner edge of the one before.

When the form is some six to eight coils high the shape should be corrected if distortion has occurred and the joins between the coils on the outer surface of the form should be welded over if they are not to be left as a decorative motif.

If the form is a divergent one it is advisable at this point to damp the uppermost coil with a little water, cover the top inch of the pot with a strip of polythene sheeting and allow the lower parts to stiffen. If too great a weight of clay is built up without this stiffening the lower parts can slump out of shape. When the lower coils are just sufficiently stiff to support a considerable increase in weight, remove the polythene from the mouth of the form and continue, as before, to add coils to the still soft upper rim. The stiffening process should be allowed to take place at regular intervals during the production of the piece, particularly if a full form rises from a comparatively small base or the overall shape of the pot is markedly asymmetric.

When the basic form has been completed it should be wrapped in polythene and left in the damp cupboard for at least twenty-four hours. This allows a degree of equalization of moisture to take place throughout the form and prevents uneven drying strains.

Coil pots are usually intended to be asymmetric in form since symmetrical shapes can be produced much more satisfactorily by the throwing technique on the potter's wheel. Frequently, however, basic coil pots are made up in a fairly symmetrical shape and beaten into their final asymmetric form with a paddle. The paddling process must proceed with extreme caution if it is not to split the walls of the piece; if radical modification of the form is intended it should be effected by degrees, allowing the clay to settle between beatings.

The final shaping of the outer surface of the piece may be achieved by planing off some of the clay wall with a surform blade or scraping down with a shaped flexible metal scraper. Scraping accentuates the effect of the grog content in the clay and produces a pleasantly rough surface texture.

A slightly modified coiling technique, consisting of the direct welding together of the plastic coils without the use of slurry, is also popular.

Coiling is frequently combined with slab building in one of several permutations. The most common and useful are (a) building pre-formed slabs of clay into the walls of coiled forms and (b) using a slab of clay resting in a supporting press mould as the lower part of a pot form and coiling the upper part on to it; the first coil is welded directly on to the

Coil pots can be built up from simple slab bases or from a more complex shape supported in a press mould (see page 57). Weld the coils together both inside and outside the form. A piece of wood may be used to 'paddle' the form into a controlled shape. The form and surface may be refined when the clay has stiffened to a leather-hard state, using scrapers and surform blades.

slab where it has been cut off at the mouth of the mould. This latter technique allows widely flaring forms to be made that would be impossible by the orthodox method.

Coiling is also ideal for building up large sculptural forms. These can be constructed in exactly the same way as pot forms or a former can be made out of card or paper and the coil form built up around it. When the form is complete the former can be crumpled inwards and removed.

Clay bodies containing considerably more than 15 per cent grog and including the coarser grades may be used for these large pieces. The diameter of the coil is also normally considerably larger than for the finer pot forms.

Slab building

Slab building is an extremely flexible technique. Forms ranging from the precisely geometric to the highly organic are possible. One can also, if necessary, work to a very large scale, which makes this technique particularly popular for architectural and sculptural pieces.

The essential qualities for a clay body to be used in slab building are: low levels of shrinkage, easy rapid drying without cracking, freedom from warping, easy positive joining, fair plasticity with good mechanical strength and no firing problems. These requirements necessitate a body formulation which combines basic clays with good workability without excessive shrinkage (such as a stoneware/ball clay mixture) with refractory materials that will keep the pores of the clay open and maintain a low average degree of shrinkage (kaolin, fireclay and grog). 2 to 3 per cent of bentonite is an excellent inclusion in a clay body for slab building as it improves plasticity considerably as well as improving the body's ability to support attentuated forms.

10 to 30 per cent of grog may be included in clay bodies for slab building.

The basis of the slab constructed form is a rolled out sheet of clay. This may be joined to similar flat panels to create a geometric plane-faced piece or the slabs, once rolled, can be joined, bent, torn, cut away or receive any of innumerable treatments to create a form of organic quality. Nevertheless, the slab pot is usually first made into a stable geometric shape, the basic structural strength of which underlies whatever modifications are later made.

PLANAR FORMS   Flat sided or geometric forms are constructed from a number of slabs joined together. Since precise results are important in this type of work the piece is normally carefully designed and cardboard templates made from the exploded drawing. In other instances only a general idea of the form exists in the mind and actual sizes and proportions are determined spontaneously in response to the apparent needs of the developing work.

In either case the following equipment (other than the possible templates mentioned above) is required: well kneaded clay of average moisture content, spacing sticks, a roller, a potter's pin and knife, slurry, a potter's sponge and a rolling board. The rolling board should consist of a reasonably large wooden or composition board about the size of a large drawing board; this is covered over with a sheet of strong hessian, canvas or close woven sacking pulled fairly taught with the edges wrapped around the edges of the board and secured underneath. (Alternatively, it is perfectly possible to roll out the clay on a length of unstretched fabric spread on a table top.)

Take enough kneaded clay to comfortably make the first slab. For small forms the thickness will be between $\frac{3}{8}$ and $\frac{1}{2}$ in. (10–13 mm), while larger forms will be constructed from slabs $\frac{3}{4}$ in. (20 mm) or more thick. Beat the mass of clay on the table until it has the approximate proportions of the slab to be made, though it will, of course, be much too small and excessively thick. Transfer the clay to the rolling board. Take the roller (which should be of the extra long wooden rolling pin type or some substitute such as a length of scaffolding pipe) and, starting from the centre of the clay, roll outwards once in each direction to the edge of the clay mass. Turn the clay over and repeat the process. Do take the trouble to turn the clay often, otherwise it binds itself to the cloth and fails to expand easily. Pay attention to the edges of the slab after each rolling; if cracks begin to appear wipe round the entire circumference of the clay with a damp sponge and eliminate them by smoothing them over with the fingers.

When the slab is approaching the necessary thickness take the two spacing sticks (these are flat slats of wood, usually about a yard or a metre long and of the thickness intended for the slab, and you will need several sets of varying thicknesses if you are contemplating any amount of slab building) and place one each side of the clay on the rolling board. The process may now continue until the roller is running cleanly along on the spacers above a slab of approximately the right proportions and exact thickness.

The template is now placed on top of the clay or the first slab is marked out on it with the potter's pin, after which it is cut out with a straight edge and the potter's knife. The slab should be put aside to stiffen while the other slabs are rolled and cut.

Having cut all the necessary slabs of clay and allowed them to stiffen a little, take the largest of the slabs, regardless of whether it forms the base or one of the sides of the proposed piece, and lay it on the rolling board or a bat. Consider which of the other slabs will be joined to the first one and where exactly the joins will be located. These joining areas must next be roughened and scored with the pin and a good application of slurry worked into the surface of the clay. The edges of the other

Large slab built sculptural form with applied relief motifs, by Keith Wallis. Height approx. 30 in. (790 mm).

53

slabs to be joined to the first receive similar treatment. (Some potters prefer to cut mitred joints between the principal constituent pieces of slabware forms.) Assemble the second slab firmly in location upon the first, making sure that the slurry forms a good join and oozes out on both sides. Using the tip or the edge of the potter's knife (or a wooden modelling tool), work the clay of the two slabs together at their point of contact so that a strong and invisible join is formed. To further strengthen this join either roll out a thin clay coil and weld it to the inside of the angle made by the two slabs or create the same effect by squeezing in some of the thick slurry, which dries to create a positive adhesion. The construction of the piece can usually continue in this way until only the top slab (and the neck, if the pot is to have one) remains.

Allow the whole construction and the remaining slab to stiffen slightly. Damp down the areas of the form to which the final slab is to be added and cover just these with strips of polythene to keep the clay moist and plastic while the rest stiffens. The part of the slab which is to complete the form should also be treated in this way. Turn it over frequently to avoid warping.

When the pot and one remaining slab are sufficiently stiff to be handled without distortion score all the areas which are to make the final join with the potter's pin and work an application of slurry into the surfaces. After a few minutes, a second, thicker, application should be made to all surfaces.

Place the final slab face downwards on the canvas-covered rolling board and lower the rest of the piece on to it, making certain that good contact is made between all the slurry-coated joints. Some of the slurry should be squeezed out as a result of the pressure exerted on it. After a short time the slurry will stiffen and the joint on the exterior of the form can be welded over with a wooden modelling tool. (Any irregularities cut into the surface of the piece as a result of this welding should be immediately filled with an excess of slurry. The surplus can later be removed with a scraper to restore the plane surface.) Roll a thin coil and weld it along the joins on the interior of the form. This is sometimes impossible due to the shape of the piece, in which case a long wooden tool must be inserted through the orifice in the pot and the interior joins welded together as well as possible.

The whole piece may be left in position on the rolling board to stiffen for an hour or two. If possible, pack the interior of the form with damp crumpled newspaper and turn the pot over on to a slatted wooden tray. Wrap the whole assemblage and wooden tray in polythene sheeting and allow moisture to equalize within the piece for twenty-four hours. The polythene may now be loosened to let in a little air. Let the pot dry very slowly in this way for several days before removing the plastic and newspaper completely.

The final scraping down of the clay surface may now be undertaken while the clay is still leather hard. Scraping clays that contain considerable amounts of grog produces a rich coarse-textured surface. It also emphasizes that the material is a clay body despite the geometry of the form.

IRREGULAR SLAB FORMS   In addition to the precise geometric type of slab pot described above there are less formal slab techniques which offer equally effective results. Of these the most common is the pot formed by bending one large slab of clay and joining the overlap to create a more or less cylindrical form. A separate slab is cut and welded to the first to form the base. Further slabs may be added to the walls to build up a large form.

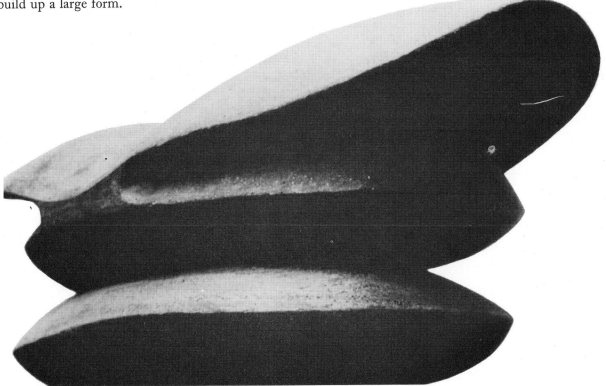

Large slab cylinders to be used as the basis for sculptural forms may be made by pressing rolled slabs of clay around a former and assembling them when stiff. The ideal formers are large size unglazed industrial clay drainage pipes, made of porous red clay and up to 6 in. (about 150 mm) in diameter, which are both cheap to buy and easy to obtain. Roll out a large clay slab as previously described and cut it to give the height required of the cylinder. Next measure the outside circumference of the clay former and cut two slabs from the prepared one, each half the circumference of the clay former in width. Press each of these

Part of a slab built sculpture made by luting together press moulded modules in various combinations. Large slab forms may be strengthened by including alumina-silicate fibre in the clay body. Width 32 in. (850 mm).

The drape mould

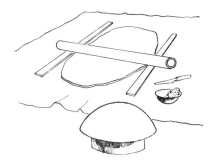

Roll out a slab of clay to the required thickness, using wooden slats as guides.

Drape the clay over the mould and cut away the surplus. A thrown form can be added with slip.

Drape moulds give plenty of scope for adding relief decoration to the exterior of the bowl form. Add decoration while the basic form is still soft and supported by the mould. Remove the bowl from the mould as soon as it is stiff enough to support itself. Stand the bowl on its lip on a flat board to continue drying.

slabs around separate formers, ensuring good contact at all points. When the slabs are sufficiently stiff to be handled without distortion pull them free of the formers, score the edges to be joined, coat with slurry and join carefully as previously described. The large cylinder formed in this way can either be stretched, paddled, cut and scraped into a sculptural form or it can be used as a superstructure to which other elements are added.

Moulded forms

Plaster of paris or fired biscuit moulds are simple to make and extremely useful for the production of a wide variety of forms from simple dishes to complex sculptures.

There are two basic types of mould – the positive or drape mould and the negative or press mould.

DRAPE MOULDS   The drape mould is a shaped hump of bisquit-fired clay or plaster, over which a slab of clay is pressed until it stiffens and takes on the shape of the mould.

The drape mould itself may be made by modelling an appropriate form from clay containing about 30 per cent fine grog. After this has dried to a leather-hard condition remove the clay form from the board and scoop out some of its interior with a sculpture tool. Allow the hollow form to dry out thoroughly and then bisque fire it in the normal manner.

A better type of drape mould is made from plaster of paris. Carve a negative of the basic shape from a slab or stiff clay using gouges of appropriate shape. This rough interior shape may then be refined by scraping off any irregularities with a flexible metal scraper to produce a negative of the form required. This may now be filled with plaster, which is left to set overnight. Release the mould by cutting away the clay which surrounds it. It is best to have the drape mould mounted off the working surface during use and this may be easily achieved by attaching the base of the mould to some stable base, such as a common house brick, with a little extra plaster.

Drape moulds are particularly useful when bowl forms are to have exterior appendages such as feet or high relief decoration or when low relief decoration is required on the inner surface of the bowl.

Make up a clay body which is sufficiently plastic to be rolled easily without undue cracking and splitting yet which contains sufficient grog and non-plastic materials to keep a low degree of shrinkage and resist tendencies to warp on drying. The clay should be used in a moderately soft state and rolled out to an even thickness as described under slab building (page 52).

Drape the formed slab of clay over the raised mould and press it into good contact, using a slightly moist sponge or a kidney shaped rubber rib. With the potter's knife trim off surplus clay hanging below the mouth of the mould and allow the clay to stiffen. Feet or other applied external forms may either be welded on to the base of the bowl at this juncture or luted on to it with slip when the clay has stiffened to leather hard. The bowl form should be removed from the mould as soon as separation is possible and it is sufficiently stiff to be handled.

Shallow designs are often carved into the surface of the drape mould, and these are transferred to the bowl as low relief decoration.

PRESS MOULDS A press mould is used when the main decorative or relief motifs are to be applied to the interior surface of the bowl. Bowl forms made in press moulds are less prone to damage during drying than those made on drape moulds, since as they dry out they automatically free themselves from the plaster form while draped bowls contract around the mould and have a tendency to split.

Make the model for the press mould exactly as for the bisque-fired drape mould. Model up a positive of the desired form on a sheet of slightly flexible material such as hardboard or masonite. Pay particular attention to achieving a perfectly smooth and uniform surface on your model and a form that is free of undercutting.

Build a wall around the completed clay hump about 2 in. (50 mm) outside the perimeter of the model at all points and about 2 in. higher than its highest projection. This wall can be made of scrap clay, wood, linoleum strip or even thick cardboard. Plug the foot of the wall and all joins against leaks with soft clay. If the mould is large, the walls should be given extra support against the pressure they will have to withstand by stacking bricks against its exterior surface.

Make up a dense mix of plaster and wait until it begins to show the first signs of stiffening. Pour about half the mix directly on to the top of the clay model. The plaster will run down the form, making good contact with all its features and forming a pool around its lower levels. It is sensible to place a piece of hessian, loose woven scrim or expanded metal on to the surface of the plaster at this time and pour the remainder of the plaster on top of it. This acts as a reinforcement and greatly strengthens the mould. Tap the table gently to bring bubbles of air to the surface of the plaster. Leave the plaster to harden overnight.

The following morning remove the retaining wall from around the mould and turn it over on to its solid plaster base. The board may be separated and removed by bending it slightly away from the face of the plaster. Cut or pull the original clay model free of the plaster to leave a perfect negative impression. Scrape, file, plane or use glasspaper to remove any sharp edges of the mould and set it aside to dry for a few days.

To make dishes in the mould, roll out the clay slab in the normal manner and drape it over the mould. Lift the edges of the clay slab and feed it down into the depression as far as it will go, finally pressing it

Making a press mould

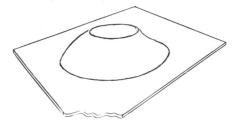

Make a positive model from plastic clay.

Construct a wall around the model and secure it with cord or wire. Leave a gap between the model and the wall. Seal the base of the wall, inside and out, with a little clay.

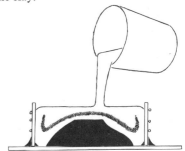

Pour plaster over the model. Hessian or expanded metal may be built into the plaster mould for additional strength.

Leave the mould to dry naturally.

Making dishes in press moulds

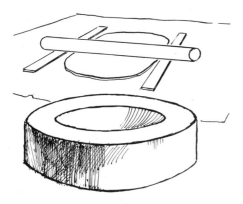

Roll out the clay to the required thickness using wooden slats as guides.

Drape the clay over the mould and gently press the clay down into it with a damp sponge, lifting the clay free of the rim to prevent it stretching and tearing.

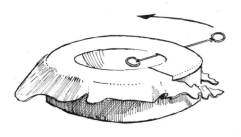

Cut off surplus clay with a potter's wire. Trim the lip of the dish and wipe it smooth with a damp sponge.

down with a sponge to make good contact with the plaster at all points. Trim off the excess clay that protrudes from the mouth of the mould with a wire or knife and allow the clay to stiffen. As the clay dries and shrinks it separates from the mould. Smooth the lip of the dish with a sponge or chamois leather and remove it from the mould by placing a board over the top of the dish and inverting it and the mould together. Carefully lift the mould away, leaving the dish inverted on the board. Allow drying to proceed with the dish in this position as it helps to prevent warping.

For deep or sheer-sided press moulded forms throw a basic shape on the potter's wheel; drop this plastic form into the mould and press into contact with the mould in the normal way.

VARIATIONS ON THE PRESS MOULDED DISH Sculptural relief may be added to the interior surfaces of moulded dishes. After the basic slab dish has been formed, and while it remains in the mould, areas may be cut out of it to create penetrations and pieces of clay slab may also be luted on to it to build up a rich relief structure. Depressions or pools may be created within this relief, which can later be filled with glaze or melted glass, while other areas can receive any of the many surface and colour treatments that are possible. Larger sculptures can be made by joining or lacing a number of these relief forms together.

Large pots and free standing sculptures can be created by joining two or more moulded pieces together lip to lip. Make one or more moulded dishes and allow them to stiffen just sufficiently to be handled without collapsing; keep them in this condition by wrapping them in a sheet of plastic while further dishes are made. When this last dish has stiffened to approximately the same degree as those in store the complete form may be assembled. Leave the most recent dish in the mould, since this helps to support its shape, and thoroughly score the rims of all those dishes or parts of dishes that are to be joined together. Work some slurry into these surfaces and allow the moisture to become absorbed into the slabs. Apply a heavy second coat of slurry immediately before the dish forms are joined lip to lip. Press the slabs together carefully to ensure a good join and use a wooden modelling tool to complete the weld. Thrown necks, for example, can also be incorporated into the design. When all the joins have been made the whole piece should be wrapped in plastic sheeting and kept for at least twenty-four hours so that the moisture content can equalize throughout the piece. Finally, the form can be refined by planing, paddling and scraping; and surface decoration and colour can be applied.

Carving

The practice of forming pottery by a carving technique is comparatively rare and the only ceramic product traditionally made in this way is the

Japanese Raku ware. Carving, however, has great potential as a forming technique because it allows the potter to escape from many of the familiar problems of slump stress, which limit the range of shapes that he can successfully produce from plastic clay, and because it allows the potter to involve himself in unfamiliar territory with new tools and develop new sensitivities.

Plasticity as such is of negligible importance in a carving clay, but in designing a clay for carving it is convenient to create a body which combines a fair degree of plasticity with a reasonably coarse and open grained texture and low average degree of shrinkage. The types of clay (ball clay, earthenware clay, bentonite) which contribute the qualities of plasticity to a clay body are those which also give it green strength, that is to say strength in its dry and semi-dry unfired state, essential in a carving clay if it is not to crumble hopelessly when worked. Thus a reasonably plastic clay containing 30 to 40 per cent grog and non-plastic materials is recommended.

Make a basic form from the malleable clay. The form should be a thick, generalized mass that conforms only approximately to the form desired, but is sufficiently full to contain all the intended modulations of the piece within its profile. While the basic form should be bulky enough to allow a considerable degree of cutting into the surface it should not be much larger than necessary since the process of carving clay is comparatively slow and laborious compared with the more common pottery forming techniques.

The basic forms for small bowls may be produced by a simple pinched technique while larger pieces may be created by beating a large mass of clay into a variety of shapes with a heavy paddle until a stimulating form emerges. Parts of this, including an interior form, can be cut out using a large sculpture tool while the clay is still plastic. In both cases the basic form, once made, should be left to stiffen a little so that it may be handled freely and is able to withstand the onslaught of knives, gouges and other cutting tools. Of course, an almost infinite range of possibilities for creating basic forms preparatory to carving exists between these two quoted examples.

The standard method of procedure is to work on the exterior form first and bring this to a state of virtual completion before attempting to carve the form of the interior. The inside walls of the basic form should be kept moist with occasional dampings while attention is concentrated on the exterior. This allows the carving of the interior to be accomplished comparatively easily, essential since the deep cuttings in the exterior walls can create strains in the clay which would not withstand the same vigorous treatment on the inside walls.

The carving technique is capable of producing pieces ranging from extreme, almost imperceptible subtlety through to the most aggressive, virile and self assertive. It is a technique not easily learned and considerable patience and involvement are demanded. In particular, it changes the potter's rhythm of working, reduces the rate of his output and elevates tools to a level where sensitivities have to be developed at the end of a blade as well as in the hands. Perhaps most important of all, it allows the potter time to reflect on his product and his processes which often serves to clarify his creative concerns.

Throwing on the potter's wheel

GENERAL PRINCIPLES Throwing is probably the most common production technique used by the studio potter. Normally it is used to create symmetrical bowls, jars, teapots, cups, flower containers, bottles and other functional hollow ware, but it can also be adapted to provide components for the creation of constructed sculpture and the formation of asymmetric hollow ware.

Any discussion on throwing should perhaps separate the highly developed skill of a practised craftsman from the problems of learning to throw. The skilled thrower almost always has an idiosyncratic technique which he has developed as a result of such factors as his height, strength, size of hands, types of wheel and clay habitually used and the kind of form usually made. Add to this variables deriving from the technique he was originally taught and subjective tastes and predispositions in such matters as the use of tools and throwing aids and one can immediately see that the permutations are virtually infinite. These highly personal techniques are usually the result of a long process of development during which the potter has probably tried numerous solutions to each of the many problems of throwing and gradually compiled a complex of movements, hand positions, sensitivities and reflexes which work for him. Now, although we can only applaud such a highly developed personalized skill, it must be highly questionable whether any potter should attempt to teach students to throw the way he does it, since it is almost certain not to suit them. Unfortunately, the problem is increased by the fact that most of what one teaches is based on what one has personally found to work. Throwing in any case takes most people a considerable length of time to learn and some depth of involvement and sheer hard work are indispensable. It therefore seems important that we teach a throwing technique which is as neutral as possible (that is to say, as free of personal mannerisms as possible) and one which makes rapid and comprehensible progress possible. The technique described below seems to satisfy these two requirements without inhibiting the later development of personal solutions. It is not, it must be emphasized, the way to throw, but only a proven way of quickly learning the fundamental processes of throwing and understanding what one is attempting to achieve by separating out the problems for individual consideration.

Throwing is very much a synthesis of mental and physical processes. Coordination is one of the most important lessons to be learned and a relaxed mind and body are also important. Tension robs you of your fluidity of movement, upsets your timing, tightens the muscles and thereby diminishes the sensitivity of your reaction to the clay. One of the main problems for the beginner is that he works much too hard, expending effort where none is necessary and thereby actually creating problems. The key to throwing is to understand the aims of each stage in the process and to develop a simple, economical and highly disciplined method of achieving the necessary result.

Potter's wheels come in many designs. At some one stands to throw, at others we sit, while many Oriental-style wheels best suit a kneeling or squatting position. Wheels may be driven by electric power (insensitive, but it does save a great deal of physical work), constant foot treadle action (these take considerable getting used to and the constant leg action has a detrimental effect on balance and steadiness in the meantime), intermittent treadle action, kicking or manual turning (this is the Japanese hand-wheel type and is unusual in that it turns in a clockwise direction). In the West, wheels normally rotate counter-clockwise. On balance, seated wheels seem to be preferred to the standing type and the sensitivity and natural rhythm of the kick wheel preferred to electric power.

Throwing clay needs to be plastic, moist and have excellent workability characteristics. It should have a degree of porosity, yet combine a non-abrasive smoothness with sufficient tooth to allow you to feel the form. It is best to learn to throw with a tried and reliable throwing clay rather than experiment with a private composition; there will be plenty of time for personal research at a later date and learning to throw in any case presents enough problems without adding an unsuitable clay to them.

Knead the clay thoroughly to remove trapped air and check that it is moist and plastic without being sticky. Divide the clay into pieces the size of average oranges and pat into neat round balls. (Do not allow either confidence or pessimism to suggest either large or very small balls of clay at this stage.) Cover with a moist cloth so they do not dry out.

You will need the following tools:

a small bowl of cold water

a potter's sponge (also known as an 'elephant ear' sponge)

a potter's pin

a potter's knife

a wooden rib (optional)

a small piece of chamois leather

a flexible cutting wire about 18 in. (460 mm) long with a handle at each end

Take your place at the wheel, make sure your position is comfortable and relaxed and that the height of the wheel is suitable for you. Most potters prefer to have most of their torso above the level of the wheel head.

The wheel head itself may be made of metal or designed to take a plaster of paris head. If the head is of flat metal, pots may be thrown directly on it, but it is preferable to attach a round bat to it. The wheel head may have studs on its surface designed to hold an asbestos bat in position; alternatively an asbestos or plaster bat may be attached by wiping the wheel head over with a little thin clay slip and pressing the bat down into a central position on the wheel head. The bat quickly absorbs the water from the slip, resulting in a positive bond.

When throwing on metal heads the clay should be dry when attached to the wheel; but asbestos bats should be wiped over with a damp sponge and plaster bats with a wet sponge.

Although the process of throwing is ultimately fluid and continuous it can be divided into stages, each of which has a specific purpose and product. For ease of understanding they have been separated below. Remember, however, that once you are able to accomplish each stage, smooth organic transition from one stage to the next should then be your first priority. Regular practice is essential and do not feel that you have to produce pots during the first few sessions. Learning the process is the first essential; without it no worthwhile product will ever follow.

PRELIMINARY STAGES

1 Wheel at rest. Damp the bat lightly, place the ball of clay in the exact centre of the wheel and press it to make good contact.
2 Wheel speed: very slow. Beat the clay into a cone with simultaneous blows from both hands.
3 Wheel speed: moderate. Press a little clay from the base of the cone down on to the bat to ensure the clay is firmly attached.

REFINING THE CONE

4 Wheel speed: maximum. Wet clay and hands. Lock hands together, brace arms on the rim of the wheel, place the locked hands on the clay and lean gently on the clay until you feel the pressure from the irregularities in the cone subside.

ALIGNING THE LAMELLAR PARTICLES ('CONING UP')

5 Wheel speed: maximum. Wet hands and clay. Close hands around the clay and apply pressure with the part of the hands nearest the bat, thus constricting the clay somewhat. Draw the hands slowly upwards while diminishing the aperture between the hands so that an attenuated cone is formed. While the lower parts of the hands are applying pressure it is the task of the upper fingers and thumbs to keep the cone revolving steadily and centrally.

6 Wheel speed: maximum. Wet hands and clay. Place the left hand around the clay – at this stage the left hand restrains and restricts the shape of the clay. With the right hand, push the clay cone down into the area delineated by the palm of the left hand. The right hand should move along an imaginary line from the right shoulder to the centre of the bat.

7 Repeat stages 5 and 6.

8 Neaten the shape of the clay mass into a centralized disc.

There are two basic shapes that one has to learn to throw and all others are an extension or a combination of these two. One should first concentrate on learning to throw the cylinder form and follow this with the bowl, which requires more precise visualization and coordination.

THE CYLINDER

9 Wheel speed: maximum. Wet hands and clay. Open up the centre of the disc. Wrap the restraining left hand around the clay disc and place the left thumb on the centre of the disc. With the right hand take the left thumb as shown and, using it as a tool, push it down into the centre of the disc until about $\frac{1}{2}$ in. (13 mm) above the bat.

10 Continuation of stage 9. Push the left thumb horizontally across towards the palm of the left hand, thus opening up the clay.

11 Working now on the trailing side of the form (i.e., the right hand side with a wheel revolving in a counter-clockwise direction), smooth any distortions in the ideal form upwards with the right hand while the left hand supports the inside shape.

12 Consolidate the lip of the form.

13 The thick low walls of the cylinder have now to be pulled up into high thin walls by a series of pulls. As the height of the cylinder increases, the wheel speed should be reduced to counteract the effects of centrifugal force. It is also advisable to throw the cylinder in a slightly tapered form until the desired height has been reached. Before you start the pull try to visualize exactly the shape you expect it to produce. The task of the left hand, operating on the inside of the form, is to draw this intended shape in space and support the clay against the pressure exerted by the right hand as it models the clay up against the drawing being made by the left hand. The relative positions of the hands during the pull are important. The left hand should start its movement at the interior base of the cylinder, the right at the shoulder between the bat and the clay wall. These positions must be maintained throughout the pull. Wheel speed: fast. Wet hands and clay. Take supporting/drawing position with the left hand. With the right hand apply firm pressure into the base of the clay wall, sufficient to make an impression. Once the impression in the outer wall has been made the two hands rise slowly

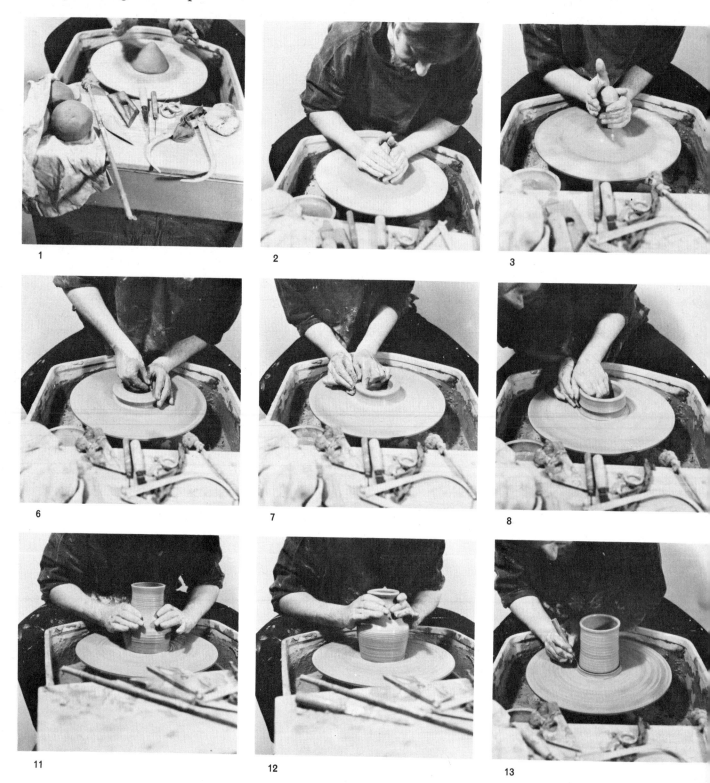

1

2

3

6

7

8

11

12

13

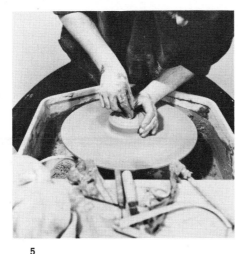

4

5

9

10

14

15

Throwing the cylinder

Equipment:

Wedged clay wrapped in damp cloth
Sponge on stick for removing excess water
from the interior of deep forms

Ribs	Chamois leather
Potter's knife	Calipers
Potter's pin	Elephant ear sponge
Cutting wire	Bowl of water

1 Place the clay in the exact centre of the bat. With the wheel revolving very slowly beat the clay into a cone with simultaneous blows from the palms of both hands (stage 2).

2 Consolidating the cone with gentle pressure from both hands locked together (stage 4.)

3 Closing the hands around the clay to cone up (stage 5).

4 Taking the cone down into a disc (stage 6).

5 Opening up the centre of the disc (stage 9).

6 Opening up the interior by forcing the left thumb horizontally across the disc towards the palm of the left hand (stage 10).

7 Correcting the distortion in the exterior of the disc, caused by the opening up process, by gentle upward pressure with the sponge (stage 11).

8 The first pull: inside hand supports the form, the other hand applies pressure at the base of the disc (stage 13).

9 Completing the first pull: stop pulling just below the rim and consolidate the form.

10 The second pull, showing an alternative position for the fingers (stage 15).

11 and **12** Necking in a cylinder to make a bottle form. Apply gentle pressure with both hands, gradually constricting the clay into a narrower cylinder. Necking in also thickens the clay which may be pulled up for extra height or modelled into a profile.

13 Separating surplus clay from the base of the pot with the potter's pin (stage 17).

14 Cutting the surplus clay free, using the potter's knife held horizontally across the face of the bat (stage 17).

15 Cutting the pot free with a twisted wire or nylon line (stage 17).

Throwing the bowl

Centre the clay and cone it as for the cylinder; bring it down into a basic disc.

Curve the base of the bowl.

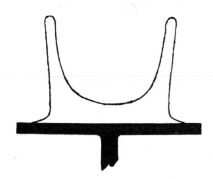

Thin the walls and pull them up.

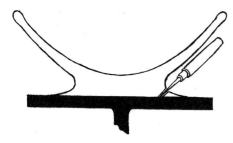

Flare out the walls to become extensions of the curve; smooth the edge of the bowl with damp chamois leather and cut away surplus clay at the base. Leave the bowl on the bat to stiffen before cutting and lifting it free.

upwards on their predetermined paths, thereby thinning and extruding the form. Do not carry the pull out through the top of the cylinder. Stop just below the lip and allow the right hand to catch up with the left. Hold this relaxed position for one or two revolutions of the clay.

14 Consolidate lip of form as in stage 12.

15 Repeat stages 13 and 14, each at a slightly slower wheel speed.

16 Refine the lip of the fully formed cylinder. If it is irregular remove a strip from the revolving form with a potter's pin and form a new lip.

If at any stage the cylinder flares outwards or if, after the full height has been achieved, the cylinder is to be converted into a bottle form, 'neck' the clay into a convergent form. Do not try to change the diameter too radically too quickly.

If on the other hand part of the form needs to be bellied outwards the right hand now takes on a supporting and drawing role while the left hand applies pressure from the inside.

REMOVING THE CYLINDER FROM THE WHEEL

17 Cut away the excess clay at the base of the cylinder. Cut through the base of the pot across the face of the bat with the potter's wire and lift the pot off the bat, using both hands with the fingers well spread to distribute the pressure.

THROWING BOWLS

1–8 Stages 1 to 8 are identical to those for throwing the cylinder, except that at stages 7 and 8 a rather wider disc should be formed than is suitable for a cylinder.

MODELLING THE BASE

9 Wheel speed: maximum. Wet hands and clay. Open up the centre of the disc with the fingers of the right hand. The right thumb moves up the vertical exterior wall to restrain its tendency to wander out of form. This may need to be repeated several times before the desired curvature of the interior is achieved. Consolidate the lip after each pull.

PULLING UP THE WALLS

10 Take up a hand position on the exterior of the disc exactly like that used to pull up the walls of a cylinder, applying some pressure inwards. The inside hand should begin its movement from the centre of the bowl, following the line of curvature, simultaneously with the near vertical movement of the right hand. When both hands emerge on the walls of the bowl the left should trail slightly behind the right, thus ensuring that a curve, albeit an uneven one, rather than an angle is maintained at the shoulder. As soon as the shoulder of the form is past the left hand must accelerate past the right into the cylinder throwing position and the rest of the height achieved in this way.

Left Modelling the interior base of the bowl (stage 9).

Above Pulling up the walls of the bowl (stage 10).

ACHIEVING A REGULAR CURVATURE

11 The onus of achieving a regular curvature, which is the prime objective in throwing bowls, lies with the left hand. Its task is more complex than for the cylinder and is a combination of three activities: (a) assessing the curvature of the base of the bowl, (b) drawing a curve for the walls of the bowl which are a satisfactory extension of the base curve and (c) modelling the curve for the walls against supporting pressure provided by the right hand. Wheel speed: slow to medium. (Speed decreases with wide diameter or shallow bowls.)

Wet hands and damp the clay. The left hand begins the assessment trajectory across the base of the bowl while the right hand waits below the shoulder of the form. The left hand is not applying any modelling pressure at this time. As the left hand approaches the shoulder the right moves off up the form so that it passes through the

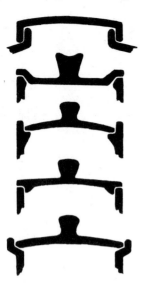

Simple lid and cover designs.

shoulder passage marginally ahead of the left. By the time the left hand reaches the change in curvature at the shoulder it should be moving strongly but slowly along a line of curvature, the direction of which has now been established. As it encounters the clay wall it takes up the process of modelling the plastic material back towards the intended curve while the right hand supports the clay against the pressure from inside and prevents general distortion of the wall. Since the modelling pull usually has to make quite an extreme modification to the existing shape of the piece, this is normally accomplished in two pulls rather than one. This prevents any possibility of tearing the clay and also allows the second pull to be much more accurately drawn since it is encountering less resistance. Finish the lip of the bowl with a chamois leather.

REMOVING THE BOWL FROM THE WHEEL

12 Some of the excess clay at the exterior foot of the bowl may be cut away with pin and knife as previously described and the bowl cut free of the bat with a wire. It should not, however, be lifted off until the clay has stiffened as bowls are particularly prone to distortion. Bat and bowl should therefore be removed together.

TRIMMING THROWN FORMS   The throwing process, while it is capable of producing highly refined forms, invariably leaves the base of the pot rather crudely formed. The refinement of the base, if desired, is accomplished later by a trimming process.

After throwing is complete and the clay has stiffened, the pot is removed from the bat and slowly dried to a leather-hard condition. In this state the pot has considerable mechanical strength and can be safely handled without distortion.

For a quick and simple method of trimming, turn the pot over and place it on its rim in the centre of a damp plaster throwing bat on the potter's wheel. Turn the wheel very slowly and test the placement of the pot for centrality by holding a finger or marking tool against the side wall of the piece. If gapping occurs between the marker and the wall of the pot for part of the revolution then the pot is off centre and has to be moved towards the widest gap that occurs between the wall and the marker. When the pot is revolving centrally stop the wheel and, holding the pot in position, secure it to the bat with three small balls of clay.

Special attention should be paid to three factors involved in the design of the foot area:

Stability. It is important that the pot stands securely on its foot after turning. This is largely determined by the width of the footring and by the area of the ring which makes contact with the table surface. Since this point of contact should be as small as possible it is usual to give a rounded profile to the base of the footring.

Above Pulling a lip. This must be done while the form is still quite soft. Support the rim with the index and second fingers of one hand and with one (or two) finger(s) of the other hand stretch the rim into a lip with firm but gentle strokes.

Above left Throwing off the hump is a technique popular in the Far East. Pots are thrown from the top of a large mound, or 'hump', of clay rather than centering a separate ball of clay for each item.

The hump may consist of as much as 30 lb (12 kg) of clay but, since the method is particularly suited to the production of small pieces, a mass of about half this amount is more normal. Beat the wedged and kneaded clay into a reasonably regular and approximately centred hump on the wheel bat. The summit of the hump alone is coned, centred and thrown into the pot form. The pot is cut free with a wire and lifted off. This process continues until the hump of clay has been exhausted.

This method of throwing is economical both in terms of time and effort.

Below left Pulling a handle from a thick coil of well wedged clay. Grasp a section of clay coil in the left hand and extrude the handle by drawing it between the thumb and fingers of the right hand. Lubricate the right hand freely with water. Bend the extruded shapes and leave them to stiffen for about an hour. Trim them with a knife and attach to the scored areas of the jug with a little stiff slip or slurry.

The basic forming techniques

Trimming thrown forms

Opposite Trimming the cylinder. Invert the leather-hard cylinder and centre it on the wheel head; secure it to the bat with three small balls of clay. Many types of trimming tools may be used. First trim the exterior of the footring and then cut out the centre recess. Finally shape the profile of the foot. Use a damp sponge or chamois leather to smooth the completed footring.

Above left and right Trimming the bowl. Centre the bowl on a slab of plastic clay attached to the bat to protect the lip during trimming. Hold the bowl in place with three small lumps of clay. First shape the exterior of the foot, taking care to produce a shape which 'grows' naturally out of the bowl form. Finally trim out the interior of the base to form the footring. This area should be modelled to reflect the curve within the interior base of the bowl. Use one hand as a rest for the other at delicate stages of the operation.

Below Trimming the bottle. Bottles and other narrow necked forms are trimmed in a chuck (a simple thrown flared cylinder of clay which has been bisque fired). Most potters keep a number of chucks of various shapes and sizes to suit different pots. Centre the chuck, attach it to the wheel and set the bottle in it. Soak the chuck in water and line it with a little plastic clay to provide a firm seat.

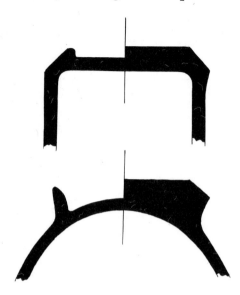

Trimming the feet of thrown wares. The right-hand side of each diagram shows an approximate section through a thrown cylinder and a bowl at the end of the throwing stage; on the left are typical solutions to the design problem of trimming.

In both cases the foot should be trimmed to approximately the same thickness as the walls of the pot.

There should be an aesthetically pleasing transition between the form of the pot and the form of the footring. The profile of that part of the pot within the footring should relate to the profile opposite it within the piece. Rounded feet tend to enhance the stability of the pot. Some pots are grasped by the footring during the glazing process; if this is intended it will influence the design decisions taken as to the form of the foot made.

Consistency of form. One of the most common causes of drying and firing faults is the presence of uneven thicknesses of clay within the form. For this and for aesthetic reasons the profile of the area within the footring usually follows that of the interior of the form.

Many small bowls and cylinders are glazed by being held by the foot and thrust downwards into the glaze. If this glazing technique is contemplated the footring must be designed so that a good and easy grip on it is possible.

First trim off any irregularities that occur on the sides of the foot area. Select an appropriately shaped and sharp trimming tool and, holding it rigidly, allow it to make one or more fine cuts up the rough part of the form, removing irregularities in much the same way as wood or metal are turned on a lathe. When the side profile has been unified the base itself may be trimmed. First, turn a completely flat foot on the piece by making a horizontal cut across the base to remove any irregularities. The actual footring itself should next be demarcated and the area inside the footring recessed back. Finally, round off the foot so that it will make the most stable contact possible with the surface on which it will stand and smooth it off with a moist sponge or chamois leather.

Refinements of the trimming process consist of covering the wheel head or bat with a slab of clay before placing the form on it, or of throwing up a clay chuck to hold the form during trimming. Both techniques protect the lips of forms being trimmed. Some potters prepare a series of thrown chucks to suit a variety of forms and bisque fire these before use. These fired chucks are sometimes lined with a layer of plastic clay before forms are set into them.

4 Decorative processes

The application of decoration is one of the stages in the production process which presents the potter with some of his most profound problems, not least of which is to question the necessity for decoration at all. Having committed himself to a form the potter has set precedents which must condition everything else that he may do or add to it. Certainly he should not think of decoration as being automatically applied to each and every piece; some pieces are deliberately designed as a vehicle for decoration, others seem to need it, while others are certainly better for being free of it. It is essential then that there is a process of assessment of the qualities, character and needs of each piece before any form of decoration is applied to it. If, as a result of this careful and deliberate consideration, it is decided that some decorative motifs are necessary then the type of addition to be made must be chosen with care so that it complements the form; also, it must be executed with an economy, decisiveness and sensitivity that is not only in keeping with the pot but which also reflects the sensibilities and thought processes generally inherent in the potter's art.

Brushwork

Brushwork is the most illustrious of all forms of pottery decoration and it is certainly one of the most famous features of Far Eastern ceramics. The decorations applied to the Chinese T'zu-chou wares, many Korean wares from the Yi dynasty and medieval Japanese potteries must rank among the finest and most noble examples of brushwork. Brushwork is certainly the most difficult and demanding of all the decorative processes and knowing the high standards of the past against which we shall be judged tends to inhibit rather than free our hands.

Brushwork decoration at its best demands subtle and dextrous physical control coupled with a disciplined mind and a high degree of aesthetic sensitivity. Practice is essential as is a complete identification with the brush and the task in hand.

The brushes are important. You must have total familiarity with the kind of mark each makes and the range of possibilities which each affords. Brushes must feel right in the hand; indeed they have to become a part of your hand and an extension of your mind. Try out a wide variety of brushes, including some home-made ones. You will find that you have a more immediate relationship with any tool that you have

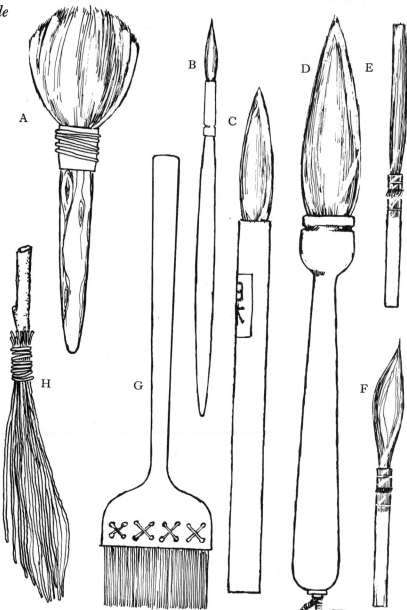

Brushes for decorating and glazing:
A slip or glaze mop
B Majolica pencil
C fude – for brushwork decoration
D large fude – for brushwork decoration
E square liner
F cut liner
G hake – for laying glaze, slip or colour
H homemade Hakeme brush for slip-
work decoration

made to fit your own hand and suit your own needs. Take care of your brushes, clean them, smooth them into shape after use and hang them up so that the hair is not damaged.

The best colours for brushwork application are the most basic and simple ones. Many natural earths and earthenware clays are suitable once they have been ground down to a fine powder form and mixed with water to the consistency of thin cream. These give a range of natural earth colours which in their unpretentiousness harmonize with honestly made clay forms.

Other colours, of course, can be obtained, preferably by grinding up local earth minerals in a ball mill and, if necessary, mixing with a little white slip, but they can also be bought from the commercial ceramics supplier. The prepared oxides of metals, each of which offers a distinctive colour after glaze firing, are commonly used for brushwork decoration, either by themselves or after mixing with slip.

The consistency of all materials used for brushwork must be modified to suit individual preferences, the type of effect required, the absorbency and texture of the surface to which it is being applied and the type of brush used.

When you have your materials prepared to a suitable condition and a brush with which you are familiar assess the needs of the piece and try to satisfy these requirements with economy and decisiveness. Commit yourself to achieving a perfect mark, that is to say to achieving an absolute concordance between your idea and your performance. Do not in any case be tempted to retouch; this compromising of personal principles of honesty to yourself, your materials and processes is both short sighted and ultimately destructive.

Slip decoration

Slip, besides being used for brushwork decoration, can be adapted to a number of other decorative techniques. Of these the most common is the application of a coat of coloured slip over all or part of a piece, either to eliminate the colour of the clay from which the piece is made or to give a two-tone effect. This process, known as 'dressing', should be undertaken when the clay has reached a near leather-hard condition. The appropriately coloured slip should be mixed to the consistency of thin cream and applied to the piece either by pouring the slip briefly into or over it or by brushing on a generous application with a wide flat hake type brush. In any case it is important that your application be executed surely and quickly so that the piece is not saturated with liquid for any length of time, as this could well cause the pot to split.

Although slip decoration is best applied to leather-hard clay it is also possible to use it on plastic and dry clay. Slip for use on plastic clay can usually be made very simply from slurry by adding water and whisking it with a paint mixing attachment held in an electric drill. It is unlikely that all the lumps of slurry will be dispersed by this action and the mixture should be run through a 40-mesh lawn. Slip for use on plastic clay is normally of a slightly thicker consistency than that for use on leather-hard and dry clay.

Colourants may be whisked into the sieved slip if so desired, but it must be remembered that it is not as easy to obtain precise and repeatable results in this way as it is when compounding the slip from dry materials.

Opposite Fungoid Forms with nepheline syenite glazes, by Peter Simpson. Height of largest approx. 7 in. (177 mm).
Photo: Derrick Witty

SUGGESTED FORMULATIONS FOR SLIPS FROM DRY MATERIALS

For application to leather-hard clay

	per cent
Calcined kaolin	5
China clay	20
Ball clay	25
Nepheline syenite	15
Flint	20
Anhydrous borax	5
Talc	5
Tin oxide	5

For application to dry clay

Calcined kaolin	22
China clay	12
Ball clay	15
Flint	20
Nepheline syenite	15
Anhydrous borax	5
Talc	6
Tin oxide	5

Substitute 20 per cent feldspar for the nepheline syenite and talc content in either composition for temperatures in excess of 1200°C or a low temperature leadless frit for the nepheline syenite for the lower earthenware temperature range.

SUGGESTED COLOURANT ADDITIONS FOR SLIPS

Add to a white slip base

	per cent
Medium blue	1 cobalt oxide
Medium green	3 copper oxide
Medium brown	5 iron oxide
Black	3 iron oxide + 3 manganese dioxide + 1 cobalt oxide
Yellow	8–10 vanadium stain
Medium grey	2 iron chromate
Tan	2 iron oxide

Speckled slips can be obtained by adding 3–5 per cent coarse granular ilmenite or manganese.

COMBING   Many varied and interesting effects can be obtained by the combing process. The pot should be dressed with a layer of clay slip of contrasting colour, as previously described, and left until it begins to stiffen. Comb through the layer of dressing to reveal the colour of the

underlying clay. This process makes an interesting surface relief decoration as well as revealing a colour contrast but is only successful as a decorative motif when it is applied with verve and confidence.

SGRAFFITO Sgraffito is a more precise but related technique and well suited to creating controlled linear decoration. Dress the leather-hard clay with a layer of contrasting slip and allow it to stiffen. Using a scribing tool or a fine 'V' gouge, cut the decorative motifs into the surface of the pot so that the clay below the dressing is revealed. By controlling the depth of the cut, elegant variations in width of line can be obtained.

TRAILING The decoration produced by trailing coloured slips on the surfaces of clay forms is a particularly attractive use of this material since it tells us explicitly about the nature of slip and its physical characteristics. It is pleasing not only to the hand that applies it but also to the observer who is able in a very direct way to re-create the consistency and flow of the slip as well as the rhythms and gestures of the hand instrumental in its execution.

Slip may be trailed directly on to semi-stiff clay forms but a thin coat of slip applied before trailing will allow the trailed clay to integrate itself into the surface of the form rather than assuming an exaggerated profile upon it.

Slip trailers are of two basic types. The first normally consists of a rubber bulb which holds the slip and a nozzle through which the fluid is squeezed. Normally the nozzle is removable to facilitate easy charging and cleaning. The other type of slip trailer is of a traditional Japanese design and consists of a large section of bamboo which acts as a reservoir for the slip, while a smaller bamboo tube leading off the main one directs the gravitational flow of slip.

MARBLING Slips of contrasting colours can be used to create interesting random marbled decoration on the interiors of bowls and dishes. The slip for marbling needs to be of a fairly thick consistency so the trails of slip do not blend into one another and lose their definition; on the other hand the slip must not be so thick that it will not flow.

Pour some slip (usually the lighter colour of those to be used) into the leather-hard bowl or dish to be decorated and tilt it so that the liquid flows around the interior of the form, covering it with a thin deposit. Pour some small quantities of the darker slip on to the surface of the first. Rather than pouring in all the second colour at one point, divide it up into three or four parts and distribute these about the area to be covered. Tilt and roll the form again as before. The flow of the slip as it sweeps around the form will link up the deposits of darker material and carry them along, leaving a marbled trajectory behind. By manipulating

Opposite Predators by Alan Barret-Danes. Stoneware with sprayed slips and lustre. Width 9 in. (228 mm). Photo: Cardiff College of Art

the tilt of the bowl a measure of control over the developing pattern can be obtained. When the desired pattern has been achieved tip the bowl into a near vertical position and allow the surplus slip to run out. Wipe the edge of the form and leave the slip to stiffen. Slip marbling is an ideal form of decoration for moulded bowls and dishes since the decoration can be applied to the form while it is still in a fairly plastic condition within the mould, which obviates the problem of the wet slip imparting excessive moisture and subsequent cracking which sometimes occurs when the process is applied to dryer forms.

Impressed decoration

The impressing of motifs into the surface of clay forms while the material is still fairly plastic is one of the oldest methods of ceramic decoration and examples of great beauty and restraint can be found from the earliest times, although it was never used to better effect than in China during the Han dynasty (206 B.C.–A.D. 220).

Any object which can be pressed into the clay surface and removed to leave a decorative impression can be used, although the most common method of proceeding is to carve special stamps out of wood or plaster. (Alternatively, they may be made of clay and fired to bisque before use.)

If plaster stamps are to be made cast some plaster blanks inside paper or cardboard tubes and allow the plaster to harden before removing the paper walls. Remove the irregularities around the edges of the plaster with glasspaper and carve the intended design directly into the surface of the plaster with a tool such as a lino-cutting gouge. Remember that you are carving a negative pattern which will result in a positive print on the clay. It is usually helpful to make a test impression on a piece of scrap clay at the completion of each stage in the carving of the stamp. (Remember that clay polluted with fragments of plaster is unsuitable for firing and, since these test impressions also clear loose plaster fragments from the surface of the stamp, the scrap clay should be discarded and not returned to stock.)

More complex designs may be obtained by pressing relief objects such as engraved lino blocks or artist's wood blocks into the surface of the clay; alternatively, the clay can be rolled on a textured surface. Continuous running patterns, as opposed to single stamps, may be obtained from carved rollers.

The effects of impressed decoration are invariably subtle and can be accentuated with a colour change, the most common methods being (1) to wipe over the surface of the form with a damp sponge charged with metallic oxide, which colours the form itself but leaves the lower impressed areas uncoloured and (2) to brush a solution of metallic oxide into the impressions left by the stamps and allow to dry, then remove the oxide from the surface of the form with a kidney scraper.

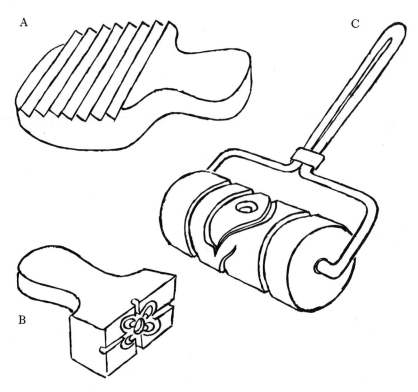

Tools used for achieving low relief decoration and texturing on wares:
A   paddle with carved surface: as the pot is beaten into shape the paddle imparts pattern or texture
B   plaster or bisque fired clay stamp with incised pattern
C   plaster or bisque fired clay roller with incised pattern

In addition to the use of stamps of various kinds, impressed decoration can be obtained by pressing combustible materials into the surface of the clay form and leaving them to be burned away during firing. Grains of rice are often used in this way in the Far East, but obviously other materials such as dried grasses, leaves, string, wood chippings and tree bark can be used.

Sprigging and relief decoration

Sprigging and relief work have elements in common with impressed decoration. Sprigging involves joining cast clay bas-relief elements onto a pot surface in the manner made famous by the English Wedgwood factory.

The technique consists of carving an intaglio motif into the surface of a small block of plaster in the manner described above. Instead of impressing this block into the clay walls of the piece, clay is forced into the intaglio under some pressure so that it picks up the full detail of the negative form. The excess clay protruding from the intaglio is cut away, leaving the clay impression within the plaster mould. As the plaster removes moisture from the clay the casting stiffens and shrinks, thereby breaking the bond between cast and mould. The cast can now be removed with the assistance of a piece of plastic clay. Score the surface of the pot where the casting is to be joined and the back of the device itself

Sprig decoration

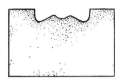

Carve or cast a negative of the sprig into a block of plaster.

Press clay into the mould and remove surplus.

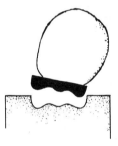

Allow the sprig to stiffen in the mould for a few minutes. Use a piece of plastic clay to remove it.

Score the back of the sprig and its site on the form. Apply a layer of slip or slurry to both surfaces and press together.

and apply a coat of clay slip to both with a brush. Press the casting gently on to the wall of the pot form and allow the slip to dry to a positive bond. Remove any slip which was exuded in the joining process with a sharp small-bladed knife.

Relief decoration on pottery can be achieved by a carving down process, by an additive one or by some combination of the two. High relief or free standing decoration is a comparatively unusual form of decoration on pottery, although it has been used to excellent effect on such wares as the Yüeh wares of China.

To create relief decoration of any height, model the clay forms to the approximate shape and proportion required and allow them to stiffen to a soft leather consistency. The pottery piece to which the relief is to be applied must be kept at a similar consistency until the relief shapes are ready to be applied. Score both surfaces and work in an application of clay slip. Press the two parts firmly together and replace the piece in the damp cupboard until the slip stiffens sufficiently to bond the two parts firmly together. The fine modelling on the relief forms may now be undertaken.

It is extremely important that these forms are allowed to dry slowly and evenly; thin parts may need to be wrapped with strips of damp cloth to retard their otherwise too rapid drying and consequent fracture.

Low relief motifs may also be created on the surfaces of pot forms by carving back the internal areas between the positive areas. If this method of achieving low relief is contemplated the walls of the piece should be made correspondingly thicker than usual. When the pot has dried to a leather-hard state use the potter's pin to incise the outlines of the positive motifs into the pot surface. Clay carving tools, gouges, trimming tools and knives can be used to cut back the background areas and reveal the relief.

Mishima

The mishima technique is Oriental in origin and, although found in the ceramics of both China and Japan, it was perhaps most expertly used by the Koreans.

In its purest form mishima consists of small scale motifs impressed into the surface of dark coloured clay wares with wooden stamps. These impressions are filled with white clay engobe and later, when the clay and slip have both stiffened, the surface is cut down with a scraper to reveal white motifs against a dark ground. In fact, mishima decoration also frequently made use of linear motifs cut into the clay with a gouge in addition to the pressed motifs and it is this form of the decoration that is most frequently used today.

Cut or press motifs into the walls of the pot in exactly the manner described for impressed decoration and allow the work to stiffen to a

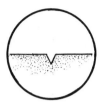

Press or cut the negative motifs into the clay surface.

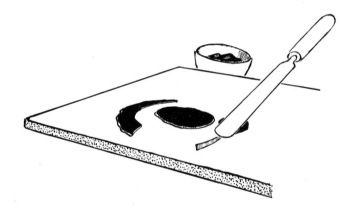

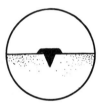

Fill the negative areas with a clay of contrasting colour.

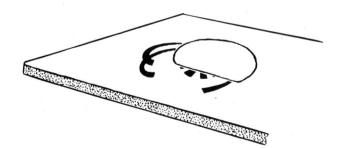

Scrape off surplus clay, leaving a sharply defined two-colour motif.

Bowl decorated by the mishima technique.
Width 4½ in. (114 mm).

leather-hard condition. Mix up the engobe with water and spread it on a porous bisque clay tile to stiffen slightly. When the engobe is semi-stiff pack it into the incised or impressed decoration, forcing it well down into all the cavities but also leaving some excess piled above the general surface of the form. Wrap loosely in plastic and allow the piece to dry slowly for about forty-eight hours. Using a metal scraper (a clay plane may be used on flat faced forms), first shave off the excess engobe until the dark colour of the base clay becomes visible between the elements of the pattern. From this point proceed with great precaution, scraping gently and cleanly across the face of the inlay until a cleanly contrasting decoration is obtained. The contrast in colour will in any case increase after firing.

Mishima inlay can be stained to any colour by including metallic oxides in the proportions suggested in the section on slip decoration; alternatively, clay body stains may be used in the proportions recommended by their manufacturer. Normally, however, mishima work is glazed over with a coloured transparent glaze which imparts a colour to the white slip but makes comparatively little modification to the colour of the dark clay base.

Neritage

Neritage is a Japanese technique for forming pieces of pottery, which has a distinctive decorative appearance. The first essential for neritage is to have two clays of contrasting colours but similar shrinking characteristics. (Many potters who use the neritage technique solve this problem simply by using the same clay body for both components but staining one to a contrasting colour with a body stain.)

Wedge both masses of clay separately until homogenous and roll out slabs of each to the same thickness. Cut both slabs into strips about ¼ in. (6 mm) wide. Paint the sides of each strip with an application of thick slip and fold two strips of contrasting colour together to make a unit. Beat the unit from both sides and all edges with a flat paddle to weld the two strips of clay together. Repeat the process, building up a number of individual patterned units which can then be welded together with more slip and paddling to make up a basic form that can later be refined by carving or turning. Alternatively, the units may be welded together into a slab form within the supporting shape of a press mould. When leather hard the surface of the pot is cut, scraped or planed down to reveal the underlying pattern of interlocking colours.

A variation of the neritage technique consists of building up a thick block of units which is then sliced through with a wire to form slabs ready for use in press moulds.

Like mishima decoration, neritage work is usually glazed with a coloured transparent glaze which provides a pleasant two-tone effect.

Opposite Neritage technique. Roll out slabs of clay of contrasting colour. Cut the slabs into strips and fold together two of contrasting colour; beat the unit from both sides to weld the strips together.

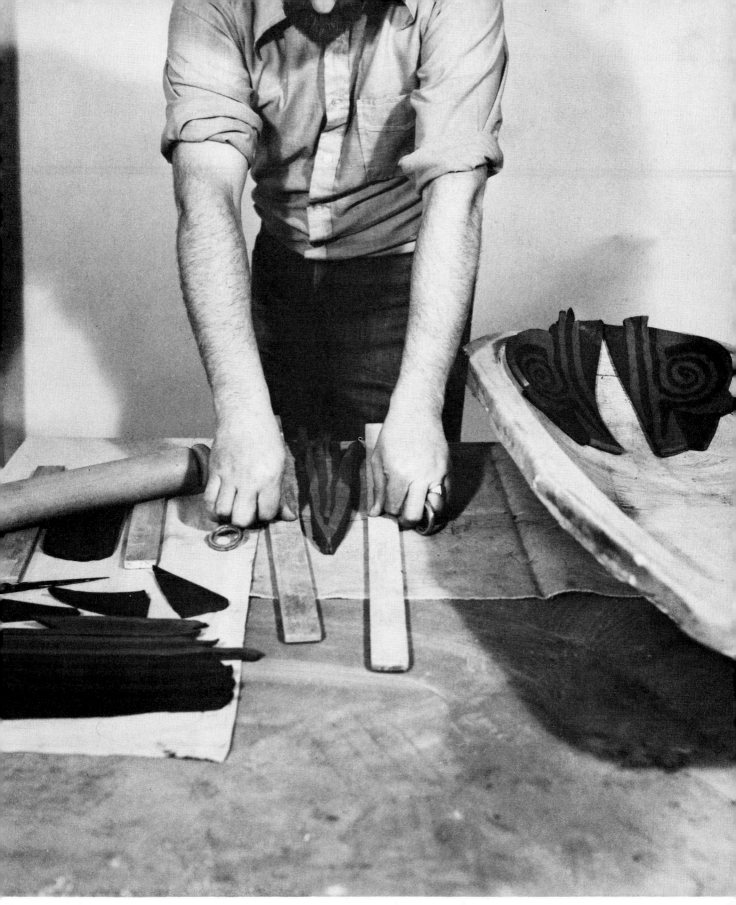

Wax resist and underglaze colour

The fact that wax resists water has been used as the basis of many decorative techniques in various crafts including pottery.

The wax most frequently used is common white paraffin wax, which is warmed gently till liquid and thinned with a little pure paraffin. Break up some pieces of white paraffin wax and place in a small saucepan over a low heat. An electric heating plate can be used, but a simple method using a candle is illustrated. When the wax has become liquid remove it from the heat and add paraffin oil (up to about half the volume of the wax) and mix. The wax should be kept liquid during use with a minimum amount of heat. The wax solidifies into a convenient solid form upon cooling and burns away when fired.

Emulsion wax resist can also be obtained from most ceramic suppliers. This is a liquid latex which requires neither heating nor thinning and is

A simple heater plate made from a cut-away lidded can is better than an electric plate for keeping wax warm.

attractive from the point of view of convenience and safety. It does not, however, produce quite such good results as the paraffin wax.

Brushes for wax resist should be kept exclusively for that purpose. A wide flat hake type brush for laying wide areas of wax and a fude for brushwork decoration with wax are both necessary.

There are two basic methods of using wax resist: the wax is used to mask the field against the colour which forms the decorative motif; or the wax is used in a positive way to form the motif.

1 Apply a broad area of wax to the dry greenware form with a hake brush. When the wax has solidified incise linear motifs through it with a scriber or fine gouge so that the surface of the form is laid bare. These patterns may now be coloured by painting over the resisted area with a mixture of metallic oxide and water; this aqueous solution is resisted by the wax but penetrates through the incised areas to stain the clay. These patterns of colour are fixed permanently by firing.

2 Use a fude brush loaded with liquid wax to lay brushwork decoration on to the pot in the normal brushwork manner. The background areas may now be coloured over with the oxide solution as before, using a broad brush or a small sponge. When the wax burns off the pot during the firing process the brushwork motifs will remain the colour of the underlying clay contrasted against the coloured background.

The oxides most frequently used to give underglaze colour are:

Cobalt:	Blue
Manganese:	Brown to plum
Iron:	Rust brown
Copper:	Green
Vanadium stain:	Yellow
Cobalt + Iron + Manganese:	Black

Mix a level teaspoon of oxide with a quarter pint of water and mix together in a jar or small container. Add two teaspoons of white slip. Mix well before use and again during use if the application is not effected quickly.

The amounts of cobalt and copper necessary to produce a good blue and green respectively may be reduced, since they are both strong colourants, while the amount of vanadium stain may need to be increased. This will depend entirely on personal preference and the depth of colour required. It is essential to test the mixtures if a controlled effect is required.

5 Drying and bisque firing

The most valuable property of clay is, of course, its tightening, from the soft plastic material of which the pot is originally formed, into a hard and durable rock-like material by the process of firing.

The vital intermediary stage between these two is that of drying. This apparently simple process is, in fact, beset with problems and finished wares must be allowed to dry slowly and evenly to avoid distortion and cracking. Particular care must be taken when drying tends to be directional, when pots are dried in the sun or in a draughty place – under such circumstances the pots should be turned round at regular intervals. Wide forms such as dishes should always be turned over to dry on their lips and all forms should be dried on slatted shelves after the trimming stage so that air can circulate to all parts of the piece. Projecting elements joined to forms – such as high relief decoration, handles and spouts – as well as rims and thin parts of the piece in general tend to dry more rapidly than the body of the pot. This sets up strains from uneven contraction and frequently results in fractures. This can be avoided by wrapping these parts with strips of dampened cloth to retard their rate of drying.

As has been previously stated, plastic clay contains a film of water between the faces of the constituent particles. As drying proceeds this film of pore water evaporates, causing shrinkage and eventually bringing the bare faces of the lamellar particles into direct contact to form a compact structure. This is the stage when shrinkage from drying has, to all intents and purposes, been completed and is termed 'leather hard', the individual particles are still damp but the lubricating film between them, which formerly allowed one to slide against the face of another, has gone. Even at this stage the pot still contains considerable amounts of water and must be further dried before it is ready for the first or bisque firing. It is difficult to generalize about lengths of drying time since they will be individual to each clay body. One can say, however, that clay bodies which are composed of small and evenly sized particles dry much more slowly than those that contain a percentage of large particles such as grog and non-plastic clays. These materials keep air passages open through the clay body as the material dries which facilitates the escape of moisture from the centre.

As clays dry from plastic to dry greenware their colour changes, usually becoming less rich. Perhaps the best test for dryness, however, is to hold the pot for a few seconds against a sensitive area of skin, such as the face or the inside of the arm. Still damp clay will feel cold and clammy while dry clay will feel comparatively neutral. After only very little experience you will become adept at gauging the drying progress of your wares by this method.

When the wares feel completely dry they are ready for the bisque firing.

The purpose of the bisque firing is to bring about the chemical reaction within the clay which irreversibly converts it to a rigid material. Even clay that has been thoroughly dried can still contain some moisture and, as its chemical formula shows, it also contains considerable amounts of water chemically bonded into the clay molecule. During the bisque firing process the remaining moisture is driven out and the chemical bond that holds the combined water is also broken, thereby allowing it to be released. Bisque firing, then, may be thought to have four stages:

1 Room temperature to 200°C: During the first 200°C the rest of the moisture held within the clay is forced out. Because the clay particles are by this time closely compacted this first stage should be effected as slowly as possible, particularly when the clay bodies do not contain much grog. If the kiln temperature rises too quickly during this stage the pressure of steam trying to force an escape route through the clay can cause the walls to burst.

2 350 to 700°C: During this part of the firing range the chemically bonded water will be released from the clay molecule. Since steam will again be seeking to force its way out of the depths of the clay, temperature rise should be slow. In fact, the vast majority of water will have been released by 500°C, but the rate of temperature increase must not be stepped up until after quartz inversion.

3 573°C: Quartz inversion from α to β (see page 32). This is a reversible process accompanied by an expansion or contraction of 2 per cent. This change in volume of quartz can also create strains that will split the clay form, so the kiln must be both heated and cooled very gradually through this temperature.

4 Up to 900°C: All clay bodies contain a number of organic and inorganic impurities as well as the many materials already existing in the form of chemical oxides. During this range of temperatures the inorganic matter will be burned out, carbon released and inorganic matter converted to an oxidized form. All these processes demand a plentiful supply of oxygen if they are to be completed satisfactorily. A lack of oxygen can cause discolouration in the bisque wares, blackening and bloating.

Packing the bisque kiln

The kiln should be cleaned before use. Remove all shelves and kiln furniture and brush out any loose fragments. The elements should be checked visually for burns and fractures and cleaned with a vacuum cleaner, avoiding all unnecessary contact with them.

Kiln shelves should be checked for cracks and the top surfaces painted with three or four coats of bat wash (50 per cent kaolin plus 50 per cent flint mixed with water to the consistency of thin cream). If the shelves have been previously painted with bat wash they may require only to have any glaze residue from previous firings scraped off and the film repaired.

Kiln shelves are made either of clay or from some highly refractory material such as silicon carbide. For firings to the higher temperature ranges the silicon carbide shelves should be used. If it is necessary to mix the two types of kiln shelves in any one firing the more refractory ones should be used for the lower levels and the clay shelves above.

Kiln furniture is of two basic types: those pieces designed to support and space the shelves and the smaller pieces which are used to carry the pieces of pottery. If kiln shelves do not rest evenly on the shelf supports a wad of refractory clay may be inserted between post and shelf.

Never fire wares directly on the floor of the kiln. A false floor of kiln shelves should be placed in the kiln, supported on refractory blocks. These supports should be located as shown in the diagram and if any other shelves are to be used in packing the kiln the supports for them should be positioned in a direct vertical line above the first ones. (Never be tempted to place supports at each corner of the shelves as this, in fact, provides less support than the method illustrated.)

It is important that wares are properly stacked in the kiln to avoid warpage and other faults. Stable forms such as bottles and cylinders may be stood directly on the kiln shelf but bowls, which are more prone to distortion, are best fired standing on their rim or lip-to-lip with another bowl of the same diameter. The foot-to-foot-rim-to-rim method of packing bisque gives a stable firing and is economical on kiln space. Small objects may be placed inside larger ones for bisque firing, but care should be taken to see that they are standing vertically. Although it is normal for the wares to touch one another in the bisque kiln and to pack as many pieces into the kiln as it will hold, the distribution of wares should be such that both heat and oxygen may penetrate freely among the wares; stacks of tiles or plates, for example, should be separated by spurs. All wares with lids or covers should be fired with these in place.

The firing temperature for bisque wares is open to a good deal of interpretation. Most potters are of the opinion that a low bisque firing followed by a higher glaze firing promotes the best possible bond between pot and glaze film. However, if a low temperature glaze is to be used on a stoneware body it will be necessary to bisque the form to near

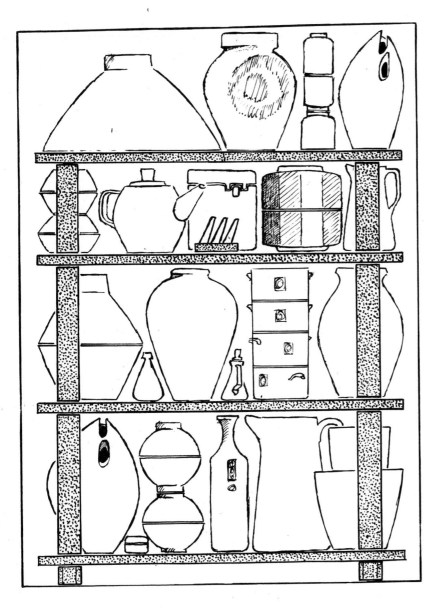

The bisque kiln. Wares may touch one another during the bisque fire so certain wares may be fired in stacks (or bungs). Larger pieces may contain smaller pieces unless they are unduly heavy for their size. Bowls tend to distort if anything other than smaller bowls are placed within them. Large bowls are best fired resting on their lip.

Avoid firing large rectangular slab pots near the elements in an electric kiln.

Pots with lids should be fired with the lids in place.

Arrange the pack so that the density of wares and shelves is fairly even in all parts of the kiln.

Make certain you can see the cones through the kiln peep-hole before you start firing. The first shelf in the kiln should be raised off the kiln floor on props and the props for subsequent shelves placed vertically above these foundation ones.

Do not allow wares on shelves to touch the kiln elements.

maturation in order to achieve a pot with suitable hardness and ring.

Bisque firing, therefore, may be as low as the point at which the oxidation process within the clay is completed and may be as high as the maturation point of the clay. Since it is difficult to apply glaze to clays that have been fired to near their point of vitrification a low bisque is preferable, except in the special case quoted above.

Normal bisque firing reaches temperatures between 890 and 1000°C. The temperature should be raised very slowly up to 575°C. Leave the door bungs open to allow water vapour to escape up to 500°C.

A safe procedure is to warm the kiln very slowly up to 100°C, then soak at minimum temperature overnight, followed by a gradual controlled rise over the next day. Allow the kiln to remain closed while it cools, a process which should take at least as long as it took to raise its firing temperature. Do not attempt to open the kiln until it has dropped to 200°C, as this can cause weaknesses in the wares from thermal shock.

The bisque fired wares should not be handled unduly and are best wrapped in newspaper to keep them dust-free until ready to be glazed.

6 The art of glazing

Glaze may be described in simple terms as a suspension of chemicals and earth minerals in water which, when deposited on the surface of a pottery form and fired to an appropriate temperature, fuses to form a coating of glass.

Glaze may be bought prepared for use or in a dry state that has only to be mixed with water. Alternatively, the potter may calculate and prepare his own glaze to suit his most precise requirements.

Glaze preparation

The dry glaze, whether bought or individually compounded, should first be passed through a 30-mesh sieve to break down any lumps it may contain. Freshly compounded glazes must be thoroughly mixed to achieve an even dispersal of the constituents. This is best accomplished in a twin-shell dry blender, but may also be done by passing the materials three times through the 40-mesh sieve with a hand mixing between each sieving. (This latter method should not be attempted without suitable protection if the glaze contains any of the raw forms of lead.)

GLAZES COMPOSED EXCLUSIVELY OF INSOLUBLE MATERIALS   Pour water into a clean non-ferrous container, sprinkle the glaze materials on to its surface and allow them a few minutes to slake. Mix the glaze thoroughly by hand until any lumps have been dispersed and a reasonably homogenous fluid has been obtained. Cover the container and leave overnight to allow the solid particles to settle to the bottom of the container and separate from the excess water. The surplus layer of water may be siphoned off the next day to leave a saturated glaze solution. Add gum solution, up to 1 per cent (gum arabic is most commonly used, but more recent innovations such as colloidal magnesium-aluminum-silicate are excellent), and mix the glaze thoroughly. A paint mixing device powered by an electric drill is fast and efficient. When a homogenous mixture has been achieved the glaze should be brushed through a 100-mesh sieve. Test the consistency of the product on a test tile made of the same clay body as that to be glazed. A brief dipping should deposit a layer about the thickness of one sheet cardboard.

GLAZES CONTAINING SOLUBLE MATERIALS   Soluble materials, such as borax, should be introduced into glazes in a fritted form. If, however, it is necessary to include soluble chemicals the compounded glaze should

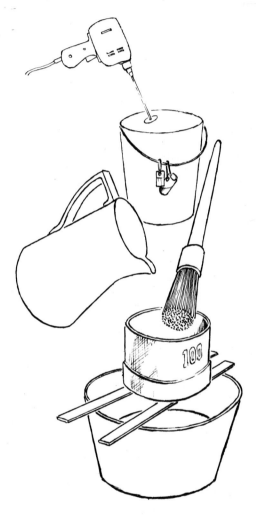

Since glaze materials settle quite quickly the glaze slip must be thoroughly mixed before use. A paint mixing attachment in an electric hand drill is good for this purpose. The glaze should also be brushed through a sieve to disperse any lumps of constituent materials or stiffened glaze.

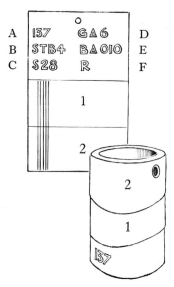

A	137	GA6	D
B	STB4	BA O10	E
C	S28	R	F

Test pots and tiles. Test all glazes under controlled conditions before using them on a set of wares. Full details of all tests, glazes, firing conditions, colourants, problems and subsequent modifications should be kept in a notebook, but since actual physical examples have more immediacy as a source of reference it is suggested that all successful tests are mounted on a pinboard and kept in the studio. It is important to know how a glaze performs on both horizontal and vertical surfaces: carry out tests on both a tile and a small test pot. Test wares should carry basic information (written on the wares with a mixture of manganese dioxide and cobalt oxide) as illustrated:

A	Notebook references (also appears on test pot)	D	Cone at which glaze test was fired
B	Clay body reference	E	Tile bisque fire temperature
C	Glaze composition reference	F	Effective kiln atmosphere during glaze firing

The tile should be dipped into glaze twice so that 1 has one thickness of glaze and 2 a double thickness. The vertical score marks on the tile demonstrate the effects of the glaze over textured areas.

be stored in a dry state and slaked immediately before use. Glaze should in any case be thoroughly mixed before use and remixed at intervals if the glazing is protracted. It is possible to overcome the problems of solubility by substituting denatured alcohol for water when mixing these glazes into a fluid slip form.

Glaze application

Glazing is an extremely subtle art and has almost limitless creative possibilities. It can be used simply to add colour and texture to a piece of pottery, but it can also be used to create mood and drama or to alter the visual qualities of the form. Your choices as to colour, glaze surface, thickness of application, the extent of the area of the pot surface you choose to cover with glaze, technique of application, etc. will all have a profound effect on the character of the piece and will either enhance or diminish its appeal. You will quickly find that scrupulous honesty to your materials creates the most favourable appearances. Glaze applied with a brush has a quite different quality from that poured from a jug. Try to discover the unique character of each method of glazing so that you can use it to its best advantage.

Wash your hands and ensure that they are free from grease before handling the wares; any grease applied to the pots at this stage will result in an imperfect glaze film.

Thick walled or porous pots should be briefly quenched in clean water before glazing. Pour water into a clean bucket, bin or deep sink and thrust the wares down into it so that both interior and exterior are quenched. Remove the pot from the water and empty as quickly as possible. Pots that have been fired to a high bisque temperature should not be quenched, even though they may have thick walls.

BRUSHED GLAZE   The application of glaze with a brush is not generally favoured in the West. It demands considerable skill and control if the brush marks are not to remain visible. Brush application is ideal when small areas have to be glazed or when a band of glaze has to be applied around a form. Although, with a little practice, glaze can be evenly applied to a small piece of pottery it will be found to be unsuitable for glazing larger forms.

Use a small brush to paint glaze into areas of undercutting or modelled detail; thereafter apply glaze to the piece with a wide, flat, soft brush of the hake type or with a glazing mop.

First apply a layer of glaze around the rim of the form and then glaze the inside of the piece. If the item is a bowl, plate or dish form start from the centre of the piece and brush the glaze outwards towards the rim. Recharge the brush with glaze after each stroke. Finally glaze the outside of the form using long, regular strokes.

It is often desirable to apply a second coat of glaze to the rim of the form.

POURED GLAZE   One of the simplest, most economical and yet reliable methods of applying glaze is to pour the fluid over the surface of the pot. This is normally accomplished in two stages, the interior being glazed before the exterior.

Pour a quantity of glaze into the interior of the form from a jug. (It is often necessary to place a funnel into the necks of bottle forms both for speed and to prevent a build-up of glaze on the inside of the neck.) Small forms may be filled to the lip and the glaze instantly returned to

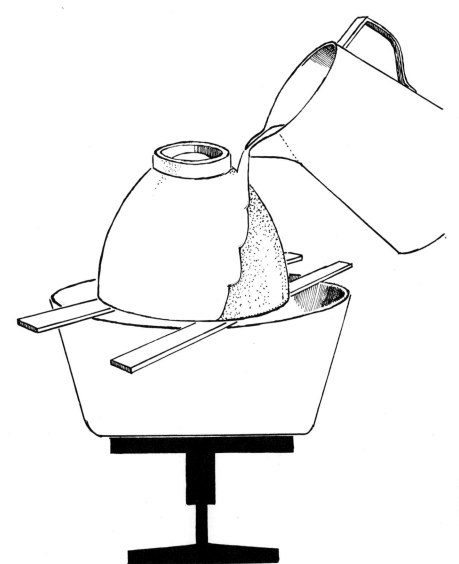

Method of glazing large or difficult-to-hold pieces. The form should be slaked in clean water and the interior glazed first. Turn the banding wheel slowly, allowing the glaze to flow down and cover the whole of the exterior of the piece.

the jug. With larger forms it is usual to pour in only a small amount of glaze in relation to the volume of the piece and to glaze the whole of the interior by rotating the piece slowly in the hands while it is held at a shallow angle just sufficient to allow the glaze to run gently from its mouth. When the pot has performed a complete revolution in the hands the whole interior surface of the piece will be glazed and the remaining glaze may be poured out more briskly. When glazing bowls by this method rotate the piece slowly while tipping it at an ever increasing angle to the vertical.

Glaze the outside of the piece by one of two methods. If the pot is of modest size and weight with a design of footring which can be easily grasped you may hold the pot in the hand to glaze. Hold the pot in an inverted position over a bowl and pour glaze from a jug on to the walls of the pot just below the foot. The glaze will flow down over the whole surface as the piece is gradually rotated to bring it into line with the glaze flow.

A number of applications of one or different glazes may be applied for decorative effect.

Bowls, large or heavy pieces or those whose design of footring will not allow them to be hand held should be inverted and placed on two rods set across the mouth of a bowl. The whole should then be set upon a banding wheel, which is turned slowly while glaze is poured on to the piece.

DIPPING   Dipping is perhaps the most common method of applying glaze and there are two simple methods by which it is done.

Combined with pouring. Glaze the interior of the piece by the method described for poured glazes. Wipe off any glaze which accumulates on the rim of the form or which runs down on to its exterior. Grasp the inverted form near its foot and thrust it down into a container of glaze so that the liquid rises up the exterior walls to the required level. Decorative effects or thicker glaze films may be obtained by one or more partial overlays.

Single dipping. Single dipping is an extremely convenient method of glazing any form, except those with narrow necks such as bottles. Dip the foot of the pot into a thin glazing resist (warm paraffin oil in which about 20 per cent by volume of white paraffin wax has been dissolved) and put it aside for a few minutes to harden. Grasp the pot firmly with a pair of glazing tongs and immerse it completely below the surface of the glaze. Hold the pot at such an angle that air pockets are not formed which would prevent the glaze reaching all parts of the interior of the form. Remove the pot from the glaze and set it aside to dry.

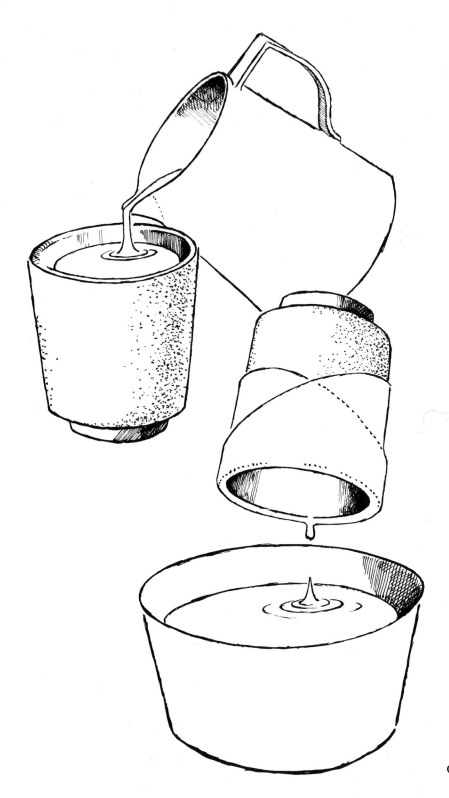

Glaze application by pouring and dipping.

It is, in fact, preferable to use the glaze in a rather thinner condition than usual when single dipping is contemplated. The wares should then be dipped once, removed from the glaze for a few moments, followed by a second application. The wax resist prevents the foot of the form from being coated with glaze.

SPRAYED GLAZE   Spraying allows the potter precise control over the amounts of glaze he applies to a given piece, but also has the disadvantages of necessitating expensive equipment and of wasting large amounts of glaze.

Spraying should be carried out only in a properly designed spraying booth fitted with an exhaust fan.

Cylinders and bottles should have their interiors glazed by the pouring method. Bowls, dishes and shallow forms may be glazed by spraying alone.

Stand the pot on a turntable within the spray booth and rotate it slowly. Direct the glaze at the pot from a distance of about 3 ft. (1 m) and keep the spray constantly in motion. If either pot or spray stops moving glaze builds up on the clay surface and, because the pot cannot absorb the water from the glaze sufficiently quickly, runs develop.

Pots that have been spray glazed need to be handled with great care since the glaze film is more fragile than from other glazing methods.

SPLASHED AND DRIPPED GLAZE   The methods described above create an even film of glaze but sometimes it may be necessary to create an irregular, informal or random effect. This can be done by splashing, dripping or dribbling glaze on to the piece. These techniques require considerable practice before they can be controlled and it is important to know how much glaze to use, from what distance it should be projected and with just how much force.

Unlike other glazing techniques, these create a distinctly kinetic appearance and can also be used to add a dramatic quality to the piece.

All or any of the techniques described above can be used in combination if required and many decorative possibilities arise from the various combinations.

It is possible to apply wax resist on top of the first glaze film and reglaze to give two-colour effects.

Paper stencil may also be used between layers of glaze to achieve two-colour effects. Apply the first layer of glaze in the normal manner. Cut stencils from an absorbent type of paper such as Japanese paper or newsprint, damp them lightly and apply directly to the glaze film. Apply the second coat of glaze and allow this to become semi-dry before probing up a corner of the stencil with the potter's pin. Pull the stencil free, bringing with it part of the glaze film.

Metallic oxides may be applied as brushwork under, between or on top of the glaze film.

FAULTS IN GLAZE APPLICATION

Pinholes or blisters. Pot too absorbent (i.e., insufficiently quenched). Treatment: when the glaze is dry rub over the surface to fill in irregularities.

Runs of heavy glaze. Too much glaze applied too quickly. Treatment: With a metal scraper, scrape off some of the glaze surface where runs have formed. Scrape up the walls of the pot, just above the foot.

Dry globules or scales of glaze or bare unglazed areas. Grease on the pot surface. Treatment: scrape or wash off the glaze and re-bisque fire.

CLEANING THE FOOT   Normally the foot of each pot must be free of glaze before firing; otherwise it will weld itself to the kiln shelves during firing. The glaze on the walls of the pot also tends to run downwards during firing.

With a clean moist sponge ~~or stiff dry brush~~ remove all glaze from the foot of the pot and $\frac{1}{10}$ to $\frac{1}{4}$ in. (2·5 to 6·5 mm) up the walls of the form. Allow pots to dry before packing into the glaze kiln.

DO NOT CREATE DUST!
SO-J

7 The nature of glaze

Glaze is a film of complex silicate compound which is fused to the surfaces of pottery wares in the presence of great heat.

Glaze is applied to the bisque fired ware as a carefully formulated mixture of chemicals and earth minerals in an aqueous solution. The water from this fluid is absorbed by the clay form which thereby causes a desposit of the solid glaze constituents to be laid upon the surface of the ware. When fired to a predetermined temperature in a kiln, this mixture of minerals sinters, then melts and fuses together to form a fluid glass which, when subsequently cooled again, solidifies and bonds itself to the clay as a glaze.

The majority of natural substances can be reduced from a solid to a liquid and eventually to a gaseous state by an increase in temperature. This change of state is reversible and gases and liquids can be returned to a solid state by cooling. Gases and liquids have no stable form but the majority of natural minerals adopt a regular structure as they become solid. This regular structure, known as 'crystalline form', is distinctive and is also the key to the formation of larger modular structures. Thus we can see that the form of a mass of a natural mineral has, in most cases, a direct relationship with the individual crystalline form. Glazes, however, do not comply with this principle. The majority of minerals from which a glaze is formulated will have individual crystalline structures, but when these minerals are fused together into a fluid glass and cooled to form a glaze neither the original nor new crystalline structures are generally formed. Glass and glaze are often called 'undercooled solutions', a term which aptly conveys this idea that glaze, though solid, has retained the structural characteristics of the fluid state.

Design and composition

The composition of a glaze has to be designed to produce the most satisfactory co-relationship between the numerous variables that are possible. These variables are largely determined by the characteristics of the following component factors:

GLASS FORMERS (ACID OXIDES) Silica is the basis of glass; it is consequently the quintessential component in all glaze chemistry. Silica can be compounded into a clay body as flint, but for glaze formulation the crystalline form known as quartz is sometimes preferred. The silica content of a glaze can also be provided by other more complex components such as clay. (Supplementary glass formers such as titanium may also be used.) From a chemical point of view silica by itself would make an ideal glaze if it were not for adhesion problems and the fact that it has a melting point as high as 1710°C (i.e., considerably higher than the maturation temperature of any clay body). Consequently various modifications have to be made to the chemical for practical reasons.

FLUXES (BASE OXIDES)   The high melting point of pure silica is brought down to a convenient level by the addition of active fluxes. The most common of these are borax, lead, talc, limestone, lithium, potassium, feldspar, sodium, magnesium and wood ash. A combination of fluxes is frequently found to be more effective in lowering the melting point of a glaze than any single flux.

BODY AND WORKING QUALITIES   A glaze composed of silica and fluxes alone would be thin, unattractive and would possess poor working qualities. A number of other substances are compounded into a glaze to give it substance or body – the most common are feldspar and clay. The inclusion of clay also greatly improves the adhesion properties of the glaze to the wares, prevents glaze component chemicals from settling too rapidly within the glaze slip and also provides a source of alumina.

REFRACTORY COMPONENT (NEUTRAL OXIDES)   Alumina is an important component in glaze formulations. It forms strong crystals of mullite in combination with silica and generally imparts strength and hardness to the glaze. Alumina assists in retarding the development of crystalline structures in glaze. As stated above, clay is the most common source of alumina in glazes.

FRITS   A number of valuable glaze chemicals that offer distinctive fluxing or colour characteristics have the grave disadvantages of being either toxic or soluble (lead, alkaline fluxes, borax, etc.). These are consequently introduced into a glaze in a convenient and stable form as a frit.

OPACIFIERS   The inclusion of oxides such as tin or zirconium will make a transparent glaze opaque or commercial opacifiers may be used. The oxides of barium, zinc and magnesium as well as those of calcium and aluminum all tend to opacify glazes in which they are included. Some opacifiers will also modify the surface texture of a glaze. Small additions of barium, for example, will usually render a glaze matt.

COLOURANTS   Colour in glazes is usually achieved with glaze stains or metallic oxides – some of these act as supplementary fluxes, others are refractory.

The components mentioned above form the basis of almost all glaze

Opposite Saltglaze pot by Walter Keeler.
Height approx. 13 in. (330 mm).
Photo: P. Macdonald

formulations although some special types of glazes may deliberately omit certain elements in the pursuit of their objectives.

The relative amounts of each basic component relate to the required working temperature and other practical and aesthetic requirements.

Common glaze types

There are a considerable number of distinct glaze types, each of which, if characterized primarily by its maturation temperature, also has the specific qualities of one of the main fluxes as its feature.

LOW TEMPERATURE GLAZES   These are designed for use on earthenware clay bodies. These bodies, which bloat and distort at higher stoneware temperatures, require a glaze which matures between 795 and 1125°C to relate to the optimum qualities of density, strength and porosity in the clay ware. These glazes may of course be applied to pots made from stoneware body, but these should have previously received a high bisque fire in order that they should have density and strength.

There are two main types of glaze which fall into this 'low temperature' category – low temperature alkaline glazes and lead glazes.

Low temperature alkaline glazes mature within the requisite temperature limits and have as their particular feature strong, clear, bright colours, particularly in the blue-green, blue and turquoise colour range made famous by the Middle Eastern and Egyptian wares of antiquity. These glazes are soft, quickly show the effects of wear, are glossy, glassy of surface and tend to craze extensively. Their chemistry is based upon the use of fluxes derived from the alkaline metals, notably potassium and sodium. Some forms of these materials also have high solubility in water, an undesirable quality in a glaze because the pot itself (unless bisque fired to maturity) absorbs considerable amounts of the dissolved alkalis during glaze application. These alkalis undergo considerable changes of volume during firing, which frequently cracks the clay form. One solution to the problem, other than the high bisque fire, is to replace the water in which the glaze is suspended with alcohol (or, less costly, to add denatured alcohol to the water in the proportion 3:2 of water), in which sodium and potassium salts are only marginally soluble.

The main alkaline fluxes are colemanite, borax, soda ash, pearl ash, nitre and lithium carbonate.

Example 1   1000°C

	per cent
Kaolin	21
Soda ash	30
Lithium carbonate	9
Quartz	39
Bentonite	1

Example 2   1060°C

	per cent
Potassium feldspar	34
Barium carbonate	14
Colemanite	41
Quartz	11

Opposite Raku bowls. Diameter 4½ in. (114 mm).
Egyptian paste necklace.
Private collection. Photo: Derrick Witty

The problems associated with soluble alkaline fluxes may be avoided by introducing them into the glaze in the form of a frit. The following range is suggested, but exact amounts and maturation temperatures will depend upon the characteristics of the individual frit.

950 to 1060°C

	per cent
Kaolin	10
Whiting	5
Soft alkaline frit	83
Clay	2

Lead glazes are the more common of the two basic low temperature types. They flow easily to give smooth, glossy, bright surfaces. The forms of lead used are white lead carbonate, red lead, litharge and galena, all of which are extremely toxic and must be handled with great care. Take care not to breathe in airborne particles and avoid mixing the glaze by hand if you have cuts or abrasions.

The problem of toxicity may be overcome by introducing the lead into the glaze in the form of a lead silicate frit (with some loss of fusibility). Lead monosilicate, lead bisilicate and lead sequisilicate – containing approximately 80, 65 and 68 per cent lead respectively – are three readily available frits. Glazes fluxed with lead frequently incorporate a supplementary flux.

Example 1   795°C (Raw lead)

	per cent
Lead carbonate	60
Borax frit	18
China clay	2
Quartz or flint	20

Example 2   1080°C (Fritted lead)

	per cent
Lead bisilicate	64
China stone	9·5
Kaolin	20
Whiting	6·5

MIDDLE TEMPERATURE GLAZES   These middle range glazes are extremely underrated. They combine the best qualities of modest maturation temperatures with stoneware characteristics. These glazes relate to the mid-range clay bodies and mature in the temperature range 1165 to 1230°C.

Example 1   1165°C

	per cent
Lead carbonate	30
Potassium feldspar	16
Whiting	9
Plastic vitrox	45

Example 2   1190°C

	per cent
Kaolin	17
Colemanite	50
Quartz or flint	32
Bentonite	1

Example 3   1190°C

	per cent
Lead carbonate	26
Quartz or flint	29
Whiting	10
Potassium feldspar	23
Sodium feldspar	5
Talc	1
Zinc oxide	6
+ Glaze gum	

STONEWARE GLAZES   These relate to stoneware clay bodies and mature in the range 1230 to 1300°C.

Example 1   1300°C

	per cent
Cornwall stone	85
Whiting	15

Example 2   1250°C

	per cent
Kaolin	15
Cornwall stone	50
Whiting	20
Quartz or flint	15

Example 3   1250°C

	per cent
Feldspar	60
Whiting	20
Quartz or flint	20

Example 4   1250°C

	per cent
Feldspar	31
Whiting	7·5
Flint	23
Kaolin	7·5
Zinc oxide	31

Example 5   1250°C

	per cent
Kaolin	25
Feldspar	49
Whiting	4
Dolomite	22

DR 32

More advanced glazes

The following glazes can be used to extend the basic repertoire and, since most of them allow room for considerable personal modification, lead to the serious professional problems of glaze design by theoretic calculation.

SLIP GLAZES   Slip glazes have a basic aesthetic appeal, both through their simplicity and through the fact that they are so closely related to the materials of which the pot is formed that they offer an appealing and fundamental sense of rightness.

In theory slip glazes consist of a single fusible clay which is applied as a slip to the unfired stoneware clay form. The ware is fired (usually into the mid-stoneware range, but slip glazes can be achieved at somewhat more modest temperatures) to the point where the fusible clay melts to form a glaze. All highly fusible clays have a high content of impurities, which limits the colour range of these glazes to black, brown and tan. If the melting point of a slip clay needs to be lowered, a flux (such as nepheline syenite or feldspar) may be added. Other materials such as colemanite may also be used. Slip glazes are normally free of the common glaze defects.

Example 1   1180°C

	per cent
Albany slip clay	88
Colemanite	12

Example 2 Temperature dependent on fusibility of the clay

	per cent
Local red clay (washed through 120-mesh sieve)	88
Feldspar	10
Whiting	2

HIGH CLAY GLAZES High clay glazes, though related to slip glazes, have the advantage of being able to use a white clay as the basic material, which consequently allows a wide range of colours to be achieved by adding recommended percentages of oxides.

Example 1185–1200°C

	per cent
Ball clay	50
Calcium borate frit	50

ASH GLAZES Wood and vegetable ashes are among the most venerable glaze materials, having been used as the principle flux in many of the finest of the world's ceramic achievements, perhaps most notably during the Chinese Sung dynasty.

Ashes should be collected, mixed and passed dry through a coarse lawn. Soak the product in water and decant the residue at two-day intervals for ten days to remove soluble matter. Screen through an 80-mesh lawn and allow to dry naturally.

Ashes of different varieties of wood and vegetables have varying degrees of efficiency as a flux and also vary in the degree with which they influence the glaze colour. In the case of ash from trees, ash derived from twigs and bark is preferable to that obtained from the solid wood.

Example 1 1250°C

	per cent
Feldspar	70
Limestone	10
Oak ash	20

Example 2 1250°C

	per cent
Feldspar	40
Limestone	2
Clay	20
Mixed hardwood ashes	38

Example 3 1200 to 1250°C

	per cent
Ball clay	18
Feldspar	40
Bentonite	2
Wood ash	40

REDUCTION GLAZES   A 'reduction glaze' is specifically designed to produce those colour characteristics typical of the kiln atmosphere in which combustion is incomplete and oxygen is in short supply. In such cases certain oxides within the glaze are robbed of their oxygen content by the hot free carbon in the kiln atmosphere; of these it is the effects brought about upon the oxides of iron and copper that are of principal interest. Instead of the tan/brown and green colours produced under conditions of oxidation iron and copper are transformed into jade green and rich copper red respectively.

Example 1   1280°C (*Celadon*)

	per cent
Potassium feldspar	79
Whiting	7
Quartz	14

+ 2 per cent ferric oxide

Example 2   1225°C (*Curtis' copper reduction glaze*)

	units
White lead	40
Red lead	40
Whiting	20
Kaolin	10
Flint	100
Borax	100
Boric acid	15
Soda ash	15
Tin oxide	5
Copper oxide	2

Firing instructions: fire smoky to 875°C, reduce strongly to 1000°C, oxidize to maturation.

Since copper reduces down to about 780°C some potters maintain an oxidizing atmosphere during temperature rise and induce a state of reduction during the cooling stage by inserting a gas torch into the kiln until the temperature has fallen below the point at which reduction is effective.

ARTIFICIAL REDUCTION GLAZES   These glazes attempt to simulate true copper reduction glazes in an oxidizing atmosphere. This is achieved by introducing extremely fine particles of silicon carbide into a suitable alkaline based copper bearing glaze. These each produce a tiny local area of reduction around themselves within the glaze mass and cumulatively impart a general effect of reduction to the glaze. Amounts of silicon carbide up to 4 per cent can be used, although the normal amounts are 1 to 2 per cent.

MATT GLAZES   The best matt glazes are the 'crypto-crystalline glazes' which develop tiny crystals on the glaze surface when they cool. These glazes need to cool slowly for the crystals to develop.

Matt effect may be induced in a glaze by underfiring, increasing the percentage of alumina or by the inclusion of barium (provided that the glaze is free of boron).

MATT RAW GLAZE FOR SCULPTURE   Spray on to dry sculptural forms and fire to 1165°C. Use thin films of glaze applied in two or three applications to retain the quality of the surface of the sculpture.

Example	*per cent*
Lead carbonate	36
Cornwall stone	10·5
Sodium feldspar	18
Kaolin	3·6
Calcined kaolin	5
Ball clay	3·7
Flint	11·5
Zinc oxide	2
Talc	1·2
Leadless frit	3·8
Whiting	2·3
Borax	1·2
Zircopax	1·2
+ Gum	

Colour examples

Black: + 5% FeO.2% Co_3O_4.2% MnO_2
Warm grey: + 3% $FeCrO_4$.2% CuO.2% MnO_2
Dull blue: + 3% $FeCrO_4$.1–5% CO_3O_4.2% MnO_2

Colouring glazes

Most glaze bases are relatively colourless although they may be opaque and whitish. Any glaze may be coloured by adding metallic oxide or glaze stain to the glaze base. Suggested additions for some of the most popular colours are given below. The amounts of oxides given are percentages of the total dry weight of the glaze base. Oxides are best compounded into the dry glaze before it is slaked into a glaze slip, but they can also be mixed into the fluid glaze.

N.B.   Variables in the composition of some materials (notably fluxes) from one deposit to another as well as reactions between the glaze and the clay body being used, or the side effects of colourants which have been included, may cause certain glazes to behave in an unexpected manner. In such a case the formulation will need to be modified slightly in order to achieve the desired results.

COLOUR	OXIDES ADDED	PER CENT	
White	Tin oxide	5	Oxidize
Turquoise	{ Cobalt carbonate	0·5	
	{ Chromic oxide	1	Reduce
Grey	Iron chromate	2	
	or		Oxidize
	Nickel oxide	1–2	
Black	{ Red iron oxide	8	
	{ Manganese dioxide	3	Any atmosphere
	{ Cobalt oxide	1	
Purple	Manganese carbonate	5	Oxidize
Burnt iron red	Red iron oxide	9	Reduce strongly
Brown	Red iron oxide	5	Oxidize
Green	{ Copper carbonate	3	Oxidize
	{ Iron oxide	1	
Olive green	Iron chromate	5	Reduce strongly
Bright red	Cadmium-selenium stain	3–5	Oxidize
Tan	Iron oxide	2	Oxidize
Yellow	Vanadium stain	4–6	Oxidize
Blue	{ Cobalt carbonate	0·5–0·75	
	{ Iron oxide	1	Any atmosphere
Brown speckle	Coarse granular ilmenite	1	
	or		Any atmosphere
	Coarse granular manganese	1	

8 Glaze firing

Glaze firing in the majority of cases reaches considerably higher temperatures than the earlier bisque fire, consequently the wares must be packed into the kiln with particular care in order to avoid damage during firing and the kiln itself must be carefully prepared.

Packing the kiln

Clean out the kiln as described on pages 89 to 90. Take extra care that no fragments of clay from the bisque fire adhere to the elements of an electric kiln. Check the kiln shelves and chip off any glaze which may adhere to them from previous firings. Repair any mars in the bat wash with a brush and, if necessary, give the whole top surface of the shelves a coat of the fluid wash. When the bat wash is dry clean off any that may have run on to the edges of the shelves.

Set the flooring shelves in the kiln so that there is an even gap between them and the kiln walls. These shelves should be set on a three-point support, unless they are very large or are to carry a very heavy load, in which case a five-point support is better. In setting further shelves in the kiln the shelf supports should be placed vertically above those that support the shelf below. Any tendency for a shelf to wobble should be corrected by placing a wad of refractory clay between the head of the supporting post and the shelf. In preparing the kiln shelves for firing do not neglect to brush off the backs of the shelves with a hand brush to remove any particles of clay or other material which may have adhered to them and could fall on to the surface of the pots below during firing.

The packing of a glaze kiln should be such that space for heat penetration is allowed between the wares, while in larger kilns the shelves should be stepped to facilitate free movement of the heat. It is particularly important not to pack wares and shelves close to elements in electric kilns; this produces hot spots which can have adverse effects on both pots and elements.

Glaze becomes a glass during the glaze firing and will attach itself to anything it touches. Pots must be placed so as to have sufficient clearance between them (about $\frac{1}{4}$ in. or 6 mm is ideal to allow heat penetration). Glaze must be wiped off the footrings of all pots and, since the glaze tends to run down vertical forms, a little way up the sides of forms. Pots

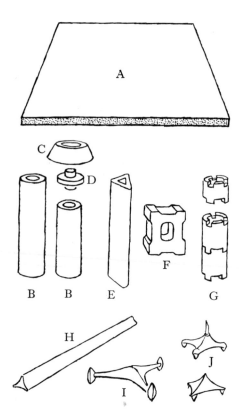

Kiln furniture:
A kiln shelf made of high-alumina clay, sillimanite or silicon carbide
B tubular props
C collar – which may be used at the base of the prop to improve stability or may be used inverted at the top to provide a larger area of support
D prop connector
E triangular prop
F rectangular prop
G castellated props
H saddle
I stilt
J spurs

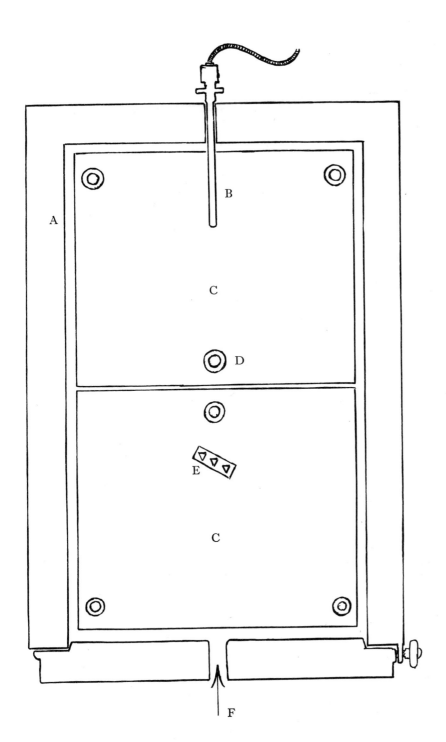

Plan of an electric kiln showing the arrangement of kiln shelves and furniture. In many kilns a prop is placed at each corner of the kiln shelf but the three-point support shown here is probably stronger.

A   insulating wall and electric elements
B   thermocouple
C   kiln shelves
D   props to support kiln shelves
E   pyrometric cones placed so that they can be seen through peep-hole F

113

may also be raised off the kiln shelf on refractory props, which are available in a variety of shapes to suit particular needs.

If pyrometric cones are to be used in firing the kiln these must be placed so as to be visible through the ports in the kiln door.

Pots should not be glaze fired until the water absorbed from glazing has had time to evaporate.

Firing

The rise in temperature over the first 100°C should be effected very slowly, after which the rate may be raised to as much as 100°C per hour.

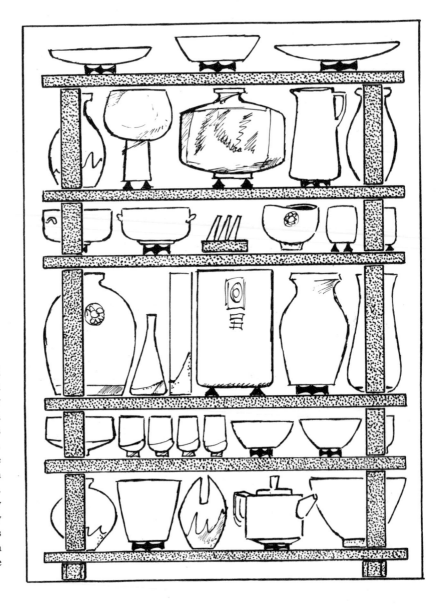

Packing the kiln for glaze firing. Glazed wares must not touch one another although the gap between them need be only very small. Kiln shelves should be coated with kiln wash. Large or geometric slab pots should be fired near the centre of the kiln. Some pots with lids are glazed so as to be free of glaze at the point of seating – in such cases the lid may be fired in place. Shelf props should be situated vertically above one another. Cones must be clearly visible through the kiln peep-hole. Wares on shelves must not be allowed to touch the kiln's elements. The density of the kiln pack should be as even as possible.

(The rate of rise should be considerably reduced for thick or sculptural wares.) The rate of temperature rise should be cut back as the maturation temperature of the glaze approaches to allow fusion to take place within it. During the last few degrees the temperature rise should be as slow as can be achieved to allow gases to escape from the glaze and for it to run smoothly. When the maturation temperature is achieved the kiln should be maintained at that level for at least one hour. This period of soak ensures the healing of all mars in the glaze caused by the release of volatile gases. After soaking, the kiln should be shut down in a completely sealed state to allow cooling to proceed slowly. The damper should be fully closed on gas kilns. The rate of temperature reduction may be allowed to increase slightly after the glaze has stiffened (100 to 150°C below maturation temperature), but dunting is kept to a minimum if cooling is effected slowly. The kiln may be opened at about 200°C.

Larger kilns have a tendency to fire unevenly and considerable experience is necessary to bring such a kiln evenly to the required temperature.

Oxidation, reduction or neutral fire

The state of the prevailing atmosphere within the kiln chamber during firing has a profound effect on the appearance of the wares. Kiln atmospheres are normally either oxidizing or reducing in their effects, although it is possible to have a condition poised between these two which is termed 'neutral'.

Electric kilns do not burn fuel within the firing chamber, no hot carbon is released from normal electric elements and there is sufficient oxygen available to allow a state of complete combustion to exist. There is no pressure on oxides within the glaze to give up their oxygen; this condition is referred to as an 'oxidizing atmosphere'.

In a fuel burning kiln, such as a gas kiln, the situation is rather different in that the actual process of burning a fuel takes place in the chamber. This inevitably releases hot free carbon. The principle characteristic of hot free carbon atoms is their intense desire to combine with atoms of oxygen to become first carbon monoxide and then, with more oxygen, carbon dioxide. As long as a fuel burning kiln is fed with an ample supply of air the hot carbon has a ready source of oxygen and an oxidizing atmosphere prevails. If, however, the burning of the fuel continues while the supply of air is cut back below the level at which sufficient oxygen is provided to effect complete combustion a reducing atmosphere is produced. The feature of this atmosphere is the presence of free carbon, which in its desperate bid to obtain oxygen from any available source now robs certain oxides present in the glaze of their oxygen and thereby reduces them to metals. Thus, while a copper bearing glaze fired in oxidizing conditions produces a green colour, a

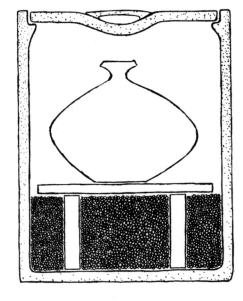

To achieve a reducing atmosphere in an electric kiln without damaging kiln elements a special saggar may be used and a local reducing atmosphere created within it. Unlike common saggars the lid must fit well and should be sealed with a graphite paste or some similar material. The lower part of the saggar is filled with a high quality and compacted granular charcoal 1 to 3 in. (25-75 mm) deep depending on the proportions of the saggar.

N.B. Kilns fitted with silicon carbide rod elements are not adversely affected by a reducing atmosphere which may be simply produced by introducing a gas flame into the kiln through one of the peep-holes in the door.

copper bearing glaze fired in reducing conditions produces the colour of the pure metal. Unless reduction effects are specifically desired kilns should be fired for oxidation as reduction has a detrimental effect on temperature rise; in any case, even a reduction firing should conclude with a period of oxidation or neutral atmosphere.

Students unused to reduction firing should not be allowed to undertake such an activity without constant experienced supervision and should in no circumstances be allowed to remove the door port plugs during reduction.

It is inadvisable to attempt to create a reducing atmosphere in an electric kiln by introducing combustible materials in the chamber since all have a most detrimental effect on the kiln elements. A reducing atmosphere may be achieved legitimately in electric kilns by replacing the Kanthal elements with silicon carbide rods (which are not adversely affected by reduction) and introducing a gas flame into the firing chamber. Alternatively reduction can be achieved within a sealed saggar fired in a conventional electric kiln – as illustrated.

Measurement and estimation of kiln temperatures

Kiln temperatures may be assessed by measurement or estimation.

A pyrometer is a device which continuously records the temperatures within the firing chamber. It consists of two connected parts, a thermocouple rod which is inserted into the firing chamber and a meter which calculates the heat level from the expansion experiences of the thermocouple. The temperature is read as a simple deflection on the meter's dial. This instrument is useful for firing small kilns, maintaining a general knowledge of the firing progress within any kiln and particularly for controlling reduction firings when other means of assessment are more difficult.

A pyrometer should not be used alone to determine glaze maturation temperatures.

A plaque of pyrometric cones. In this example the kiln is being set for a cone 8 firing; cones 7 and 9 indicate when optimum temperature is near or if over-firing should occur. The cones should be set in the sockets to lean at an angle of 8° from the vertical. At cone 8 the cones will bend as shown below. At higher temperatures it may be difficult to see the cones within the incandescent kiln, in which case blow gently towards the peep-hole of the kiln from a distance.

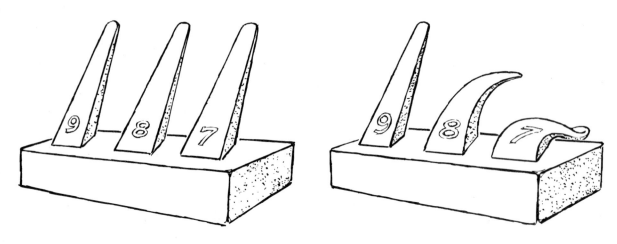

Pyrometric cones (or bars) are the most standard and reliable method of determining specific kiln temperatures. Cones are elongated pyramids of compacted ceramic material and are in fact closely related to glaze itself. Each cone has a numerical notation and its precise melting point is known. Cones covering a range of temperatures are placed among the pots within the kiln so that they can be seen through the kiln door observation ports. By following the softening and bending of these cones an accurate assessment of kiln temperature is possible.

Cones should always be used with glaze firings since their time/temperature characteristics are identical to those of glazes.

A list of cone temperatures is to be found on pages 137 to 138.

Kiln temperatures can be quite accurately assessed by observing the visible colour of the kiln's interior through the door ports during firing. This is essentially a skill based on personal experience, but a general outline is given below.

°C	*Colour*
Below 475	Black
475	First visible redness
650	Dark red
775	Cherry red
815	Bright cherry red
900	Orange red
950 to 1000	Orange
1090	Yellow
1200	Pale yellow
1300	Whitish yellow

This method of assessment is particularly useful for Raku firings and noting temperature variations within large kilns.

9 Kilns

There are numerous categories of kiln design and a wide variety of variations within each category so that it is difficult to generalize about design. Fundamentally there are two methods of heat application, which makes for a preliminary categorization. Kilns are either (a) insulated boxes within which heat is generated or (b) chambers through which heat is drawn by draught.

Electric kilns

Electric kilns are of type (a); no fuel is burned in them and they are not fitted with dampers or a chimney system. Heat is supplied from coiled electric elements of kanthal, which are usually recessed into the fire brick which forms the inner liner of the kiln. Better kilns also have elements in the floor and door surfaces. Depending on their size, electric kilns are wired with between two and five circuits, each controlled by an on/off switch. Thus it is possible to control and equalize temperatures within the kiln simply by manipulating the flow of current to the various circuits.

Electric kilns are safe, free of smoke and noxious fumes and easy to operate. On the other hand they are expensive for their capacity and very large ones do not fire well, particularly towards the centre where radiant heat does not penetrate. Repair of refractories and elements is also an expensive item. From an aesthetic point of view the most serious disadvantage of electric kilns is their naturally oxidizing kiln atmosphere. Attempts to achieve reduction in electric kilns either seriously accelerate the rate of element wear or necessitate major and expensive modifications to the kiln (such as replacing the elements with silicon carbide rods) and methods and techniques of firing.

Most electric kilns are fitted with a pyrometer and one or more thermocouples so that it is easy to keep abreast of heat rises within the firing chamber.

There are several standard designs of electric kilns but the most common are the front-loading variety and the top loader.

All electric kilns should be fitted with a switch which automatically disconnects the current when the door is opened.

Fuel-burning kilns

Given a free choice the majority of studio potters would probably choose to use wood as a fuel. The magnificent products from Oriental

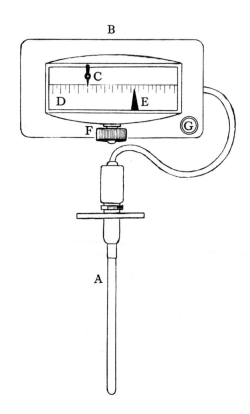

The control pyrometer:
A   thermocouple (a silica housing containing a bi-metal strip)
B   pyrometer (a potentiometer with readings translated into degrees of temperature)
C   kiln temperature indicator
D   scale (usually in 100° units)
E   pre-set maturation temperature indicator
F   pre-set temperature control knob for E
G   limit switch for automatic power cut out when maturation temperature is reached

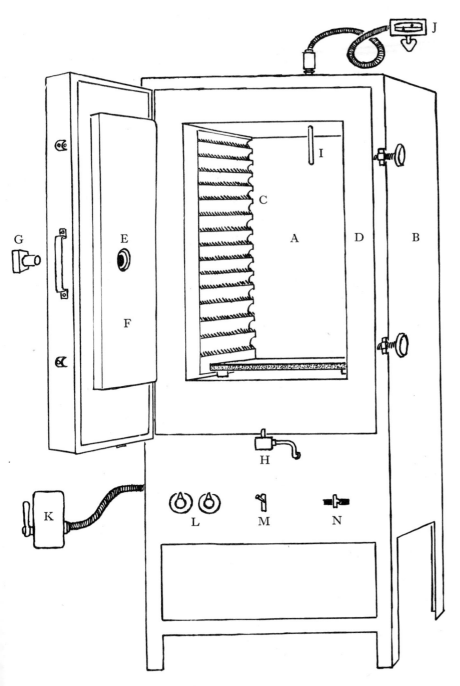

Features of an electric kiln:

A   firing chamber
B   steel bodywork
C   electric elements
D   insulating firebrick
E   peep-hole
F   insulated kiln door
G   peep-hole plug
H   automatic switch to cut off power if door is opened
I   thermocouple
J   pyrometer
K   main power switch
L   variable power control – separate for each phase
M   kiln on/off switch
N   soak/cut off control

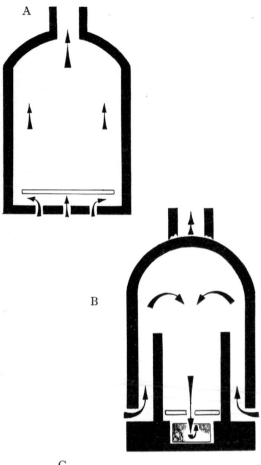

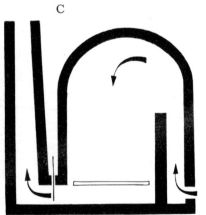

The three basic draught patterns in fuel burning kilns:
A   updraught
B   downdraught
C   crossdraught

wood-burning kilns are still considered by most of us to be the aristocrats of the world's pottery and it is this mystique, together with the incomparable excitement and rhythm of wood fire and certain unique qualities that it imparts, that accounts for its attraction. The practical difficulties, however, place this ideal medium outside the realm of possibility for most potters. Those who feel compelled to use fuel-burning kilns, therefore, usually make use of the more practical fuels of gas (mains or bottled varieties, such as propane) or oil.

Fuel-burning kilns have the advantages of being comparatively cheap to build relative to their cubic capacity, performance does not diminish with increase in size, maintenance costs are lower than for electric kilns and both oxidizing and reducing kiln atmospheres are readily available. On the negative side fuel-burning kilns lack the portability of electric kilns, they often require elaborate smoke and fume dispersal systems unless built outside and they need experienced operators if they are to be precisely fired.

The three main types of design for these kilns are updraught, crossdraught and downdraught. The principles of each are illustrated.

Fuel-burning kilns frequently have a simple 'brick up' door, often incorporate an arched roof and control the movement of air and gases as well as the kiln atmosphere with a system of dampers.

It is perhaps the flexibility of the fuel-burning kiln together with the intimacy of its operation that accounts for much of its attraction. Provided that a fuel source is readily available, they are not difficult to build or modify and indeed it is even possible to build a kiln around a particularly large or unusually shaped piece of sculpture.

Roman-style and other simple kilns

BUILD A ROMAN-STYLE KILN   This kiln is based on typical Romano-British designs but incorporates a few minor modifications. It consists of two distinct parts: permanent lower levels, and the dome which is built anew for each firing. (The line through 'x' shows the division between these two in the diagram.) The lower levels of the kiln are dug into the ground, thus providing strength and good heat insulation. Diagram 1 shows the basic dig which precedes construction of the kiln. The floor of the firing chamber area is made by pounding sherds into the earth.

The point of transition between the firebox, Y, where the fuel is burned and the interior of the kiln, Z, takes the form of a honeycomb of fired saggar clay pipes, B. Construct this honeycomb as the first stage of the building process and level off the gaps in the top layer with a stiff mixture of mud and sand.

Next construct the brick walls, W. Complete each circle of bricks before starting on the next course. Fill in gaps between bricks with the mud and sand mixture. When the brickwork is completed build up the earth mound, V, and dig the refractory bats, A, into the walls of the firebox trench and cover with earth as shown.

Construct the central support, F, for the suspended firing chamber floor and set the flooring in place. The flooring shown in the diagram is a perforated refractory ceramic material but any suitable substitution may be made for this. Pack the wares to be fired into the kiln, remembering that the pack may rise above the level of the permanent wall to the height of the intended dome. Since unglazed reduced wares are the normal product of Romano-British type kilns the pots may be stacked directly one upon the other, larger pots being placed at the lower levels. The domed stack of pots should be covered with dishes or large sherds. If the kiln is to be used for low temperature glaze wares these should be stacked in the normal manner for glazed wares (see pages 112 to 114).

The temporary dome is constructed on a framework of bent wooden supports – thin split bamboo that has been previously soaked in water for a few days is ideal – covered with a thick layer of clay and sand mix, large sherds or tiles and finally earth.

Force the bamboo supports into the earth mound so that they take up the curvature of the dome. (Note that for unglazed wares the dome can be partly supported upon the mound of wares within but for glaze firings the arch needs to be of an increased curvature for additional self support.) Bamboo supports should follow the distribution pattern shown in diagram 2A.

A stiff mixture of clay and sand together with grass or straw as a binder is laid over the framework to complete the dome leaving only the

Roman style kiln:
A   refractory bats forming the roof of the firebox
B   honeycomb of fired saggar-clay cylinders
C   perforated refractory flooring shelves (or some substitute)
D   permanent brick wall
E   earth mound
F   central support for suspended floor of firing chamber
S   smoke-vent
T   minimum curvature of dome; increase the curvature somewhat for firing glaze wares
V   earth mound
W   permanent courses of brick
Y   firebox
Z   firing chamber

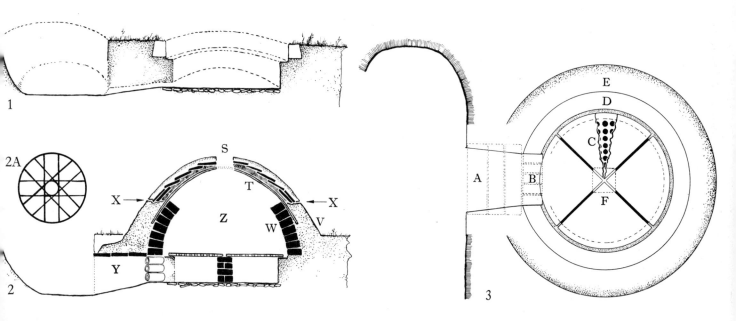

smoke vents open. Working from the lower levels of the dome upwards, press large pottery sherds or tiles into good contact with the clay dome. (Additional strength is obtained if the sherds are daubed with sticky clay slurry before being applied.) Overlap the sherds as shown in the diagram. Allow the dome time for the clay and sherds to stiffen into a compact structure and then complete the kiln with a covering of earth or turf.

The kiln is fired with wood as fuel: cut and split tree branches or industrial off-cuts. A slow preliminary firing of two to three hours duration to dry out the kiln is suggested before firing proper begins. Firing takes nine to ten hours and temperatures in the 1000 to 1080°C range are possible. The smoke vents may be totally or partially closed as a damper.

The kiln normally produces a reducing atmosphere.

The kiln may be modified to incorporate a second firebox opposite the first. This reduces the firing time and produces a more even heat distribution within the firing chamber.

BUILD A SIMPLE UPDRAUGHT FUEL-BURNING KILN   This type of kiln may be used for Raku, bisque firing, Egyptian paste, enamels, or for most types of low temperature glaze wares. It uses any of the common slow-burning solid fuels.

The structure may be made from common brick for Raku or the lower temperature ranges but if higher temperatures are contemplated or if the kiln is intended as a semi-permanent one it should be made from refractory firebrick.

The belly of the kiln is transversed by firebars which retain the fuel and support the saggar which forms the firing chamber. It is advisable to paint the interior of the kiln with several coats of kiln wash before each firing as this assists in removing clinkers.

The kiln has a main air-intake tunnel opposite the chimney which can be used to direct fire from a flame gun into the heart of the kiln for an initial lighting of the fuel. Alternatively the kiln may be lit with wood and the solid fuel gradually added. The two subsidiary air-intake tunnels assist in maintaining an even temperature within the kiln. Any or all of the tunnels may be partially closed at any time to slow the progress of the kiln, while the chimney aperture may be totally or partially closed to provide a simple dampering system. The mouth of the kiln may be covered with a metal lid for Raku firings but a closer fitting refractory bat should be used for other types of firing.

This type of kiln increases its temperature quite rapidly once well alight and additional heat from a flame gun or from forced air is seldom necessary. The most common necessity is to slow the rate of temperature rise to prevent damage to wares.

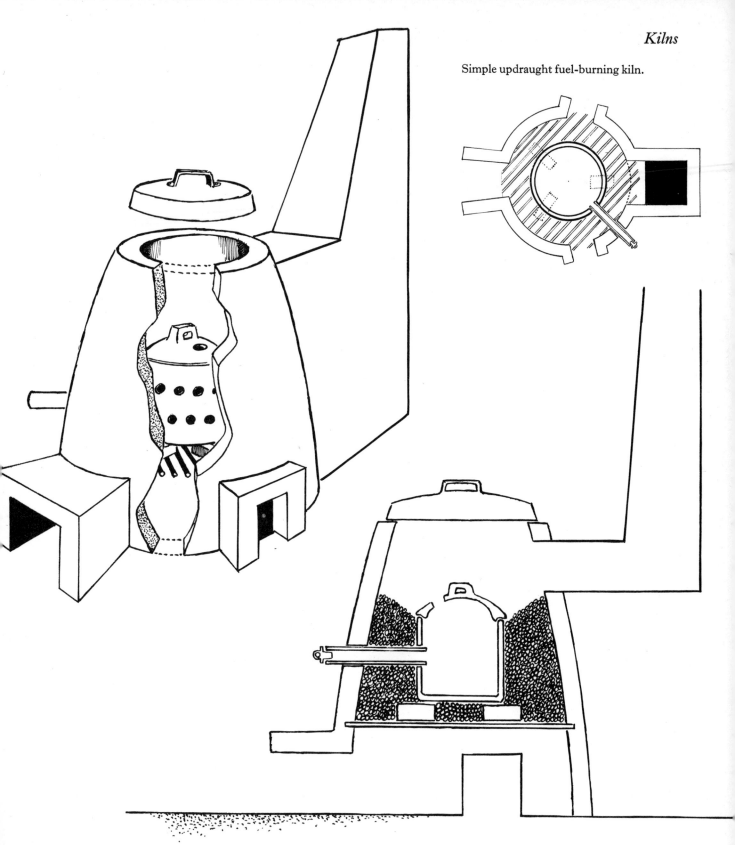

Simple updraught fuel-burning kiln.

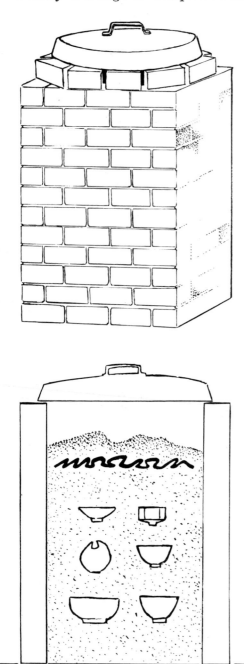

Sawdust kiln.

BUILD A SAWDUST KILN   The sawdust kiln is a remarkably simple device for firing pottery and is really only one stage advanced beyond the most primitive methods of open firing.

Wares for firing in a sawdust kiln should be made of an open textured clay containing sand or grog and they must be well dried.

The kiln is constructed from about eighty common bricks. No mortar or seal is used between the bricks; leave a gap of about $\frac{1}{4}$ in. (6 mm) for air supply. (If the kiln is in a very sheltered location the gaps between the bricks may need to be increased.)

Pour sawdust into the kiln to a depth of 6 to 8 in. (150-200 mm) and place the heaviest pots to be fired on this mound. The pots should have at least 2 in. (50 mm) between one another and between themselves and the walls of the kiln. If the pots are open forms such as bowls or cylinders they should be filled with sawdust. Cover the pots with 2 in. (50 mm) of sawdust and set in the second layer of wares. This process is continued until the lightest wares have been set at the top of the pack. There should be 12 in. (300 mm) of sawdust above the top tier of pots. The kiln is lit from the top. Soak some sacking in paraffin or oil and place it on top of the sawdust within the kiln. Cover most of this with a thin layer of sawdust and ignite the sacking. As the sawdust on top of the sacking catches fire add additional fuel until a good intensity of heat is being generated. The kiln may now be covered with a tin lid as shown.

The sawdust in the kiln smoulders, rather than burns, downwards. Much smoke is given off but if flames issue out from between the bricks of the kiln too much draught is present and the gaps between the bricks should be closed somewhat with a mixture of sand and clay. Once the correct rate of burning has been achieved the kiln will normally fire itself and burn out in between twelve and thirty-six hours leaving a pile of wares showing the direct effects of fire in the bottom of the kiln.

10 Variations and extensions of the basic theme

Salt glazing

Salt glazing was invented in the German Rhineland during the early part of the fifteenth century, where it quickly became popular and developed into one of the most pervasive styles during the sixteenth and seventeenth centuries. Although salt glazing is still popular in the Rhineland it has now become a part of the general international repertoire of ceramic techniques with practitioners in most parts of the world (see colour plate, page 103).

Salt glaze has an attractive appearance and subtlety of texture. Brown is the most common colour although blue, grey and tan are also popular. The glaze tends to be unevenly distributed over the surface of the wares and flashing from the fire is frequent; these features give salt glaze an appealing sense of uniqueness.

The basic salt glazing process involves firing the wares up to, or near to, the maturation point of the clay body, at which time salt is introduced into the firing chamber of the kiln. The heat causes the salt to volatilize and the sodium released combines with free silica in the clay body to form a glaze of sodium silicate.

In addition to its appearance one of the greatest attractions of this type of ware is the fact that it needs to be fired only once. The wares are packed into the kiln in a dry greenware state and taken through to the final glaze form in a single process. Unfortunately, however, salt glazing has a profound effect on the kiln within which the pots are fired since the interior of the kiln as well as the pots becomes coated with glaze during salting, thereby rendering it unsuitable for any future use other than salt glazing. The very fabric of the kiln also deteriorates rapidly, particularly around the fire inlet ports, and fumes of poisonous chlorine gas and hydrochloric acid are given off, all of which necessitate great care being exercised when managing a salt kiln. Good ventilation and air extraction equipment are essential for indoor salt glazing.

Pots for salt glazing may be made of any clay body that is available, although well balanced bodies should be slightly modified by having the flint content marginally increased. Free silica in the clay body is used as a glass former for the glaze during salting and the thickness and quality of the glaze coating formed is dependent upon its availability. If colours are required on salt wares they should be applied as part of a siliceous clay slip.

The salt kiln should be of a fuel-burning type of downdraught design. Many potters prefer to build themselves a simple gas- or oil-fired structure rather than turn over one of their regular kilns to this process. The lining for such a kiln should be of high silica refractory brick with additional exterior insulation provided by common brick. (High alumina refractory lining materials have recently become popular since they slow the normally rapid deterioration of kiln brick which is typical of this process.) Two particular features need to be built into the kiln. The first is a port, or ports, through which salt may be introduced into the firing chamber. This is usually done through an aperture in the roof of the kiln. A spreading device must be incorporated within the chamber below this aperture. Some potters add salt as a drip-fed solution through the sides of the kiln. The second feature is an easily opened and closed aperture in the kiln door (a single fire brick incorporated end on so that it can be easily removed is ideal) to enable sample rings to be withdrawn from the kiln during firing to test the build up of glaze.

When preparing the kiln substitute aluminum hydrate (or even aluminum paint) for bat wash since the salt would form a glaze over regular bat wash; apply to all surfaces and edges of bats, refractory props and even to kiln walls.

Pack the kiln so that there is plenty of clearance between the wares to allow the sodium vapours to penetrate to all parts of the ware. Remember that shelving will reduce the efficiency of the glazing and design and pack your kiln with this in mind.

Salt glazing is notoriously bad at reaching the insides of hollow wares, so these should be given a coating of some convenient glaze.

Salt kilns are extremely inefficient on their first few firings due to the fact that the kiln walls steal a large percentage of the glaze. It is consequently advisable to try a preliminary firing before actually glazing wares. This allows you to test the efficiency of the kiln and if an extended and heavy salting is employed on this occasion the subsequent first firing should be considerably better than one could normally hope to expect.

It is important that salt wares are fired to the maturation point of the clay body so that the silica it contains is as potentially reactive as possible.

The salt used for glazing is common rock salt and this must be soaked before use since water is a necessary part of the reaction. A set of cones should be placed in the kiln to determine the maturation temperature of the clay when salting may begin. Introduce the salt through the roof port, either loose from a long handled shovel or wrapped inside a piece of water soaked paper. The salt breaks down into a vapour almost instantly and the kiln's dampers should be almost closed so that the salt vapour does not simply escape. Salt should be added at 10 to 15 minute intervals, depending on the efficiency of the kiln design. Between eight and ten saltings are usually necessary. After the sixth and subsequent saltings open up the kiln dampers, remove the door plug and withdraw a test ring to examine the accumulation of glaze. Salting should proceed until a sufficiently thick glaze film has been achieved. Use about $1\frac{1}{2}$ oz of salt for each cubic foot capacity of the kiln for each salting (or about 150 g per cubic meter).

There is no particular operating temperature for salt glaze firing since it depends almost entirely on the maturation temperature of the clay used for the wares. Temperatures from about 1080°C up to 1300°C are used although in the region of 1250°C is the most popular.

Although porcelain is outside the general brief of this book it is worth mentioning that salt glazing can be used to marvellous effect on porcelain wares. Metallic oxides and carbonates should be applied to the wares as part of a ball-clay slip. Iron, copper, manganese and cobalt produce particularly magnificent colour effects.

The salt glazing process may be summarized as follows:

$$2NaCl + H_2O \rightarrow 2HCl + Na_2O$$
$$\downarrow$$
$$Na_2O + nSiO_2 \rightarrow Na_2O \cdot nSiO_2$$

N.B. It is possible to use soda as a substitute for salt in this glazing process. The procedure and effects are very similar but the chlorine fumes are avoided.

Egyptian paste

The Egyptians developed low temperature alkaline glazes during their predynastic period and by 3000 B.C. they were in widespread use across the kingdom. The style of pottery now known as Egyptian paste emerged as a result of the great demand for small-scale decorative ceramic items such as bead jewellery (see colour plate, page 104) amulets and small religious figures. These items were originally made from a highly siliceous and non-plastic clay containing considerable quantities of soluble alkalis such as borax. The forms were made by simple techniques such as rolling and cutting for the beads while the amulets and figures were press moulded.

Egyptian paste is interesting today for its historical associations – through it we can re-create quite faithfully the propositions implicit in the world's earliest concept of glaze – and also for its unusual technical means. From a technical point of view Egyptian paste is unusual in that the glaze components are compounded into the body in its original dry state before being slaked. When water is added the soluble fluxes are largely dissolved into the pore water. After the wares have been formed and are left to dry the evaporation of the pore water causes the soluble alkalis to migrate through the open body to the surface of the piece where they are deposited. Great care is necessary between the drying and firing stages since careless handling destroys the efflorescence on the surface of the wares, which is essential to glaze formation.

An Egyptian paste should have the following qualities:

1 high in glass forming silica and low in clay content (maximum clay: about 25 per cent)
2 largely non-plastic and porous
3 contain 10 to 12 per cent soluble sodas such as sodium bicarbonate, soda ash (anhydrous sodium carbonate) or borax
4 contain the glaze colourants within the body formulation (e.g., 1 to 3 per cent copper oxide, 0·5 to 1·5 per cent cobalt oxide, 1 to 4 per cent manganese dioxide).

A typical formula for Egyptian paste to mature at 925 to 950°C:

	per cent
Flint	18
White sand (fine)	8
Kaolin	13·5
Feldspar	39
Ball clay	3
Sodium bicarbonate	6·8
Soda ash	4·7
Borax	1
Whiting	5
Bentonite	1
+ Colourants	

Place the dry materials in a bowl and add water, a little at a time, kneading it with the hands until it becomes malleable. It is important not to allow the paste to dry out until forming is completed and it should therefore be kept tightly wrapped in plastic until used.

Egyptian paste should be modelled as briefly and as simply as possible since it is not suited to excessive handling. Beads may be rolled as a coil, then cut to length and pierced with a dampened potter's pin. Allow beads to dry standing on their ends rather than on their sides or, preferably, in their firing position. Drying normally takes about 72 hours.

For firing, the beads should be strung on nichrome wire between posts – it is important that the beads do not touch one another. Other forms may be fired on spurs or standing on a layer of sand.

Only a single firing is necessary. The kiln temperature should be raised slowly throughout and soaked for 30 minutes at maturation.

Majolica and overglaze enamels

Majolica and overglaze enamels are the two best known types of

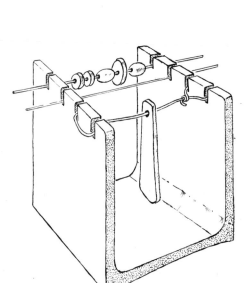

A simple firing frame for Egyptian paste, slab built from saggar clay or from heavily grogged stoneware clay. The frame can be individually built to fit your test kiln or enamel kiln but each frame should not exceed 6 in. (150 mm) in width. Modules of similar frames should be used in larger kilns.

Wares may be fired on rigid or flexible wires. Paint the wires with a little kiln wash (mixed into a paint-like consistency with a saturated gum solution) which should be allowed to dry before use.

Wares should be placed on the firing wires shortly after formation and allowed to dry there.

decoration that are applied on top of the glaze film rather than beneath it as is usual.

MAJOLICA   This technique is of Italian origin and consists of painting motifs on to the dry surface of an opaque white – or near white – unfired glaze, which decoration when fired burns into the glaze and fuses with it. The effect usually leaves some evidence of the mark of the brush and the decoration has an appealing softness due to the slight movement of the fluid glaze.

The clay bodies used for the formation of Majolica wares are traditionally low temperature white or ivory wares, maturing at about 1100°C. Since few white burning clays become resonant in this temperature a considerable percentage of flux is usually incorporated into the formulation. Of the possible fluxes feldspar is most commonly used, but calcium compounds are more authentic. A typical body would consist of:

	per cent
China clay	20
Ball clay	30
Whiting (100 mesh)	30
White sand (very fine)	20

Alternatively, a buff Majolica body using feldspar as a flux might conform to the following guidelines:

	per cent
China clay	25
Ball clay	23
Red clay	2
Flint	30
Feldspar	20

After the bisque fire the form is given a coating of opaque white glaze (traditionally a lead/tin glaze), which should in itself be featureless since its sole purpose is to act as a background for the brushed decoration. The essential feature of this glaze must be that it is modified very precisely in relation to the firing temperature so that although it fuses to form a smooth glaze it does not flux sufficiently to flow down the form and thereby destroy the precision of the decoration.

White background glaze for segar cone 05a (1000°C)

	per cent
Lead bisilicate frit	75
Feldspar	12·5
Flint	12·5
+ 5 per cent tin oxide	
+ gum or sugar	

The gum or sugar, in different ways, harden the surface of the glaze when it is dry so that it is possible for a brush loaded with colour to work on its surface and apply as involved or elaborate a pattern as may be desired. The overglaze colours themselves, although normally applied quite precisely with a brush, may be applied in any suitable manner.

Commercial underglaze colours mixed with gum and a little of the background glaze base (i.e., without the tin oxide) provide an easy and convenient method of achieving a satisfactory decorating material. Alternatively, more personal colours can be prepared from mixtures of oxides (50 per cent) and the dry background glaze base (50 per cent), ground together with a muller and brought to a glutinous paste with alternate single droplets of water and saturated gum solution. Thin this mixture with water, if required, at the time of use. Apply colour with a well loaded brush.

Fire the kiln as for an earthenware glaze firing with a short period of soak at maturation.

N.B. Much traditional Majolica was raw glazed and fired only once. Although this increases the risk of damage during the decorating stage it is a perfectly acceptable practice, but firing must then proceed at the more leisurely pace used for bisque firing.

OVERGLAZE ENAMEL   Unlike Majolica, overglaze enamel is applied to the fired glaze surface and the piece is then refired to fuse the enamels and bond them to the glaze surface. Many of the more elaborate commercial enamelled wares employ several firings at the enamel stage to achieve a wide range of chromatic effects. This is obviously not an attractive proposition to the studio potter who prefers to restrict himself to a single enamel firing.

Enamels are usually applied to the surface of glazed stonewares or porcelain and earlier comments in relation to Majolica concerning the simplicity of the background glaze also apply to the effectiveness of enamel.

Technically, enamel is simply a very low temperature glaze which matures in the range of seger cones 016 to 015a (i.e., 750 to 800°C). Numerous enamels are commercially available but they can be made by combining metallic oxides (for colour) with a simple low temperature flux/glass-former mixture combined with the considerable amounts of gum necessary to make the enamel adhere to the form.

Enamel composition

	per cent
White lead	72
Flint	28
+ Oxides and gum	

Red lead is in fact slightly more fusible than white lead, but its strong colour tends to make assessment of the density of the enamel film problematic.

N.B. Since some oxides act as fluxes in addition to providing colour the basic flux mixture may have to be modified slightly for some colours in order to achieve a maturation concordance. This is most easily achieved by making slight variations in the flint content.

Enamels must be brought up to temperature and cooled extremely slowly if they are not to peel.

Fire in an oxidizing atmosphere.

Raku

The art of Raku was conceived and developed in Japan during the last quarter of the sixteenth century, specifically for the production of ceramic wares for use in the Tea Ceremony. The name 'Raku', meaning 'pleasure', was given to the descendants of the famous sculptor-potters who created those early pieces that are arguably the summit of refined aestheticism in the ceramic arts (see colour plate, page 104).

Strictly speaking, the term 'Raku' applies solely to the art and products of the Raku family Masters but it has also come to mean a ceramic technique that has been traditionally used by them. A somewhat debased version of the original technique passes for Raku in the West and, although it is a confusion of several facets of the original art and despite the fact that it in no way even approaches the fringes of the aesthetic achievements of the original, it is nevertheless one of the most involving and instructive techniques within the spectrum of ceramics and offers unique opportunities for self-development and real creative excitement.

Raku is committed to the basic premise that the pot is the product of a process of mutual interaction and refinement between man and nature and that through this involvement man discovers his own significance. Raku places great reliance on maintaining a close and intimate relationship between the pot and its maker at all stages of production, and particularly so during the moments of truth when the pot is subjected to severe and sudden ordeal.

Raku wares are made by carving and refining forms down from larger leather-hard ones which have been raised by the pinching technique.

The clay used for these wares is coarse, open pored, refractory and highly resistant to thermal shock. The following are three typical compositions:

		per cent
1	Stoneware clay	60
	Mixed grog	40

2 Stoneware clay	24
Plastic fireclay	24
Ball clay	12
Grog (30 mesh)	12
Sand	28
3 Local brick clay	35
Sand	30
Stoneware clay	28
Ball clay	5
Bentonite	2

If Raku forms are made using the joining techniques, particular attention must be paid to welding the parts into a totally unified structure. Otherwise the wares will later split apart under the stresses of thermal shock.

One of the most popular Raku colours is a rich salmon red, achieved by basting the leather-hard form with several coats of ochre slip. Oxides and other forms of decoration may also be applied in the normal way. After careful drying the wares should be bisque fired to a temperature of 850 to 900°C. It is important that Raku bodies never approach their maturation temperatures during firing.

Raku glazes are traditionally simple in their basic chemistry although they are used with great subtlety. They are of a lead-boro-silicate type, which is usually interpreted in the West as a fritted glaze for the purposes of safety.

Typical Raku glaze compositions:

	per cent
1 Calcium borate frit	75
Sodium feldspar	15
Lead sequisilicate	10
+ Gum	
2 Calcium borate frit	80
Sodium feldspar	20
+ Gum	
3 (Toxic glaze)	
Lead carbonate	65
Quartz	20
Lithium carbonate	10
Kaolin	5

Raku glazes may be applied by any technique that suits the style of the piece, but traditionally the wares are brush glazed. Glazes should be built up into a thick and varied film on the exterior of the piece by a system of total and partial overlays. The interior should be given a simple and less thick application.

The best known aspect of the Raku process is the technique employed for glaze firing. This is normally carried out in a small and easily constructed fuel-burning kiln of updraught design. Its main features are a saggar (coiled or thrown from a Raku clay body) which acts as a firing chamber, easily removable lids to saggar and kiln and a viewing tube through which the potter is able to watch the development of his glazes as they approach maturity.

Raku glazes mature between 750 and 1000°C. A kiln burning smokeless fuel will normally reach this working temperature in about three hours. During this period the pots to be fired should be stood on the air intake tunnel or on the kiln lid to warm and to eliminate any vestiges of moisture.

The firing of Raku glazes demands precise, well coordinated and disciplined action if a great deal of kiln heat is not to be wasted.

Remove the kiln cover and the saggar lid with a pair of long-handled tongs or a lid hook. Grasp the pot with the tongs and set it into the

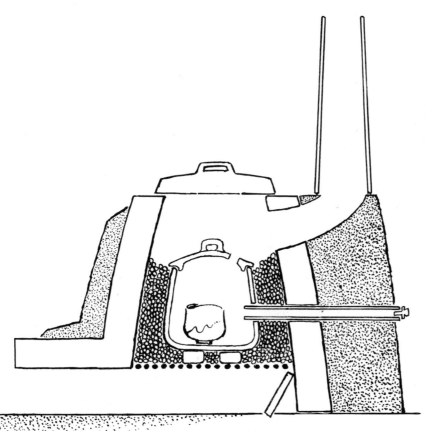

Small circular Raku kiln burning coke or smokeless fuel. The saggar is the heart of the kiln and the main wall follows its profile. The walls may be made of common brick for a temporary kiln or of firebrick for a more permanent structure. The belly of the kiln is transversed by a number of firebars which both support the saggar and contain the fuel. The rectangular air intake tunnel may be used to direct fire from a flame gun to the centre of the kiln if fast firing is desired.

The kiln may be lit either with wood and the coke gradually added from above or by means of the flame gun. The chimney is a commercial chimney pot and the whole kiln has an insulation of banked earth.

The development of the glazes within the saggar may be observed at intervals through the viewing tube which may be made of metal or clay.

The kiln will reach glazing temperature in two to three hours.

Right Building a simple Raku kiln from common brick. This small kiln has a chimney and a single air-intake tunnel. The saggar is in the centre of the kiln and the viewing tube projects out through the side of the kiln's belly. This kiln uses coke or smokeless fuel, supplemented in this case by a paraffin flamegun which is directed into the air-intake tunnel. Gaps between bricks are closed with a mixture of sand and clay.

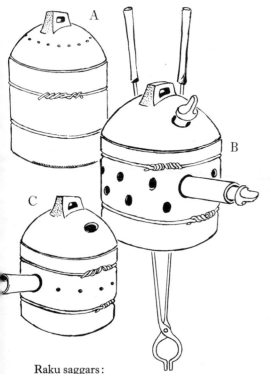

Raku saggars:
A   for bisque firing
B   for firing Raku glazes
C   for firing the special black Raku glaze in a charcoal kiln

The viewing tubes of both B and C types of saggar should be fitted with a bisque fired clay plug.

Bands of heat resistant wire around the belly of the saggar increase its life.

The tongs for setting and removing wares from the kiln should be light in weight and easy to operate.

saggar in such a position that it will be visible through the viewing tube. Replace both lids quickly.

Stoke the kiln and raise the temperature slowly until observations of the pot through the viewing tube show its glaze to be in the process of fusion. Close the chimney and air vents and allow the kiln to soak for about five minutes. The average glaze firing of any piece takes only 15 to 20 minutes to complete.

Open the dampers to clear smoke and gases from the kiln and once again check the appearance of the glaze, which should appear smooth and glossy. Again remove the cover and saggar lid. With the tongs, snatch the red hot pot, still covered with glowing molten glaze, from the kiln and drop it into a metal container filled with a combustible material such as sawdust, straw or dry leaves, which will ignite instantaneously. Cover the container and leave to smoke for some minutes. During this period the pot will experience strong secondary reduction conditions which will bring about colour changes in the glaze, produce haphazard areas of lustre and cause any unglazed areas of the pot to become a dense matt black colour. After a few minutes in the secondary reduction chamber remove the pot once again with the tongs and freeze the state of the glaze by plunging it into water.

The results of Raku firings are pots that are intensely idiosyncratic and which exhibit both the unique scars of their experience as well as the random patterns and markings which are the signature of the process. The potter likewise has experienced an ordeal and has had his involvement put to the test. He will also have achieved a new kind of rapport with glaze and fire and have extended his control over the genesis of his product in a new, fuller and more intimate way.

After quenching the pot should be scrubbed with a stiff brush and allowed to dry, at which time the full subtlety of the effects of the process will manifest themselves.

Technical appendices

Properties of the most common ceramic materials used in glaze design

MATERIAL	COMMON SOURCES	NOTES
Alumina Al_2O_3	Feldspar Cornish stone Alumina hydrate Kaolin Nepheline syenite	Neutral oxide in glazes where it controls the melt of the glaze by contributing a refractory quality, also contributes hardness and acid resistance.
Barium oxide BaO	Barium carbonate	Base oxide in glazes where it normally acts as a strong flux.
Boric oxide B_2O_3	Borax Colemanite Boric acid	Neutral oxide in glazes which can serve as a base or an acid but is normally used as a flux. Makes glazes glossy.
Calcium oxide CaO	Dolomite Calcium carbonate Colemanite Bone ash	Base oxide in glazes. Used as a subsidiary flux in low temperature glazes and a primary flux in porcelain. Increases the strength of a glaze.
Iron oxide (Ferric) Fe_2O_3	Ferric oxide	Neutral oxide in glazes where it is used as a colourant but also has a fluxing action.
Lead oxide PbO	White lead Red lead Galena Litharge Lead frits	Base oxide in glazes. Very active flux for low temperature glazes. Poisonous. Imparts a glossy surface.
Lithium oxide Li_2O	Lithium carbonate Spodumene Petalite Lepidolite	Base oxide in glazes where it acts as a flux.
Magnesium oxide MgO	Dolomite Talc Magnesium carbonate	Base oxide in glazes. Acts as a refractory at low temperatures but becomes an active flux at higher temperatures.
Potassium oxide K_2O	Cornwall stone Volcanic ash Potassium feldspar Potassium carbonate	Base oxide in glazes. Strong alkaline flux which increases the brilliance and hardness of glazes.

MATERIAL	COMMON SOURCES	NOTES
Silica SiO_2	Quartz Flint Sand Clays Feldspar Cornish stone Petalite	The primary material in the acid group of oxides for glaze composition. Combines with the base oxides to form a silicate glass.
Sodium oxide Na_2O	Sodium feldspar Nepheline syenite Soda ash Sodium chloride	Like potassium it is an active alkaline flux but has a higher coefficient of expansion. Imparts brilliance to a glaze.
Tin oxide SnO_2	Tin oxide	Acid oxide in glazes. The best of all opacifiers.
Titanium oxide TiO_2	Titanium dioxide Rutile	Refractory acid oxide in glazes. Used as an opacifier.
Zinc oxide ZnO	Zinc oxide	A useful base oxide since it contributes opacity to a glaze as well as reducing thermal expansion and crazing. Contributes to glaze strength and acts as a flux.

Conversion table for pyrometric cones, bars and rings
(Nearest equivalents)

°C	°F	BRITISH CONES	SEGER CONES	ORTON CONES	HOLDCROFT BARS	BULLERS RINGS
750	1382	016	016	017	—	—
760	1400	—	—	—	6	—
770	1418	—	—	—	—	—
790	1454	015	015a	016	7	—
795	1463	—	—	—	—	—
805	1481	—	—	015	—	—
810	1490	—	—	—	7a	—
815	1499	014	014a	—	—	—
830	1526	—	—	—	—	—
835	1535	013	013a	—	—	—
840	1544	—	—	014	8	—
855	1571	012	012a	013	—	—
860	1580	—	—	—	9	—
875	1607	—	—	—	10	—
880	1616	011	011a	012	—	—
890	1634	—	—	—	11	—
895	1643	—	—	011	—	—
900	1653	010	010a	010	—	—
905	1661	—	—	—	12	—
920	1688	09	09a	09	13	—
930	1706	—	—	—	—	—
935	1715	—	—	—	14	—
940	1724	08	08a	—	—	—
950	1742	—	—	08	15	—

°C	°F	BRITISH CONES	SEGER CONES	ORTON CONES	HOLDCROFT BARS	BULLERS RINGS
960	1760	07	07a	—	16	1
970	1778	—	—	—	17	—
980	1796	06	06a	—	—	—
985	1805	—	—	07	18	—
990	1814	—	—	—	—	—
1000	1832	05	05a	06	19	5
1015	1859	—	—	—	—	—
1020	1868	04	04a	—	—	—
1030	1886	—	—	—	—	10
1040	1904	03	03a	05	20	—
1060	1940	02	02a	04	21	—
1065	1949	—	—	—	—	15
1080	1976	01	01a	—	22	—
1100	2012	1	1a	03	23	20
1115	2039	—	—	—	—	—
1120	2048	2	2a	02	24	—
1125	2057	—	—	—	—	25
1140	2084	3	3a	01	25	—
1145	2093	—	—	—	—	—
1160	2120	4	4a	1	—	—
1165	2129	—	—	2	—	—
1170	2138	—	—	3	—	30
1180	2156	5	5a	—	—	—
1190	2174	—	—	4	—	—
1200	2192	6	6a	5	26	35
1205	2201	—	—	—	—	—
1230	2246	7	7	6	26a	—
1240	2264	—	—	7	—	40
1250	2282	8	8	—	27	—
1260	2300	—	—	8	—	—
1270	2318	—	—	—	27a	—
1275	2327	—	—	—	—	45
1280	2336	9	9	9	28	—
1285	2345	—	—	—	—	—
1300	2372	10	10	—	29	—
1305	2381	—	—	10	—	—
1320	2408	11	11	11	—	—
1325	2417	—	—	12	30	—
1335	2435	—	—	—	—	—
1350	2462	12	12	13	31	—

Defects in clay, glazes and firing with suggestions for remedies

CRACKING OR SHATTERING OF THE FIRED FORM

Likely causes:

1 Excessive absorption of soluble fluxes from the glaze. Increase the temperature of the bisque fire or modify the glaze by introducing the soluble fluxes in the form of frits.

2 The body contains too much free silica.

3 Thick glaze may have been applied only to inner or outer surfaces, thus putting pot into a state of excessive tension.
4 Too rapid cooling of a body unsuited to withstanding thermal shock. Either cool much more slowly or introduce grog into the body composition.

BLISTERS (BLEBS) IN CLAY BODY

Likely causes:

1 Air trapped in the clay body due to poor wedging.
2 Excessive amounts of body colourants included in the clay.

UNSIGHTLY WHITE DEPOSIT ON GREENWARES

This is due to the presence of soluble sulphates within the clay. Add 2 per cent barium carbonate to the clay body.

FRAGMENTS DETACH THEMSELVES FROM THE SURFACE
OF THE FIRED WARES

This fault sometimes occurs several weeks or even months after firing. It is usually due to the clay being polluted with fragments of limestone or plaster. A small bead of white material can often be seen at the seat of these fractures.

CRAZING OF THE FIRED GLAZE FILM

Crazing is a comparatively common fault in glazed wares and takes the form of a network of fine cracks through the glaze film, which can be unsightly and unhygienic in table wares.

The most common cause of this fault is excessive tensile stresses between glaze and body (normally referred to as an 'illfitting glaze'). The glaze, having a greater degree of thermal expansion than the body, contracts to a greater degree upon cooling and thereby crazes. Ideally glazes should be in a state of only slight compression.

Delayed crazing may also occur due to subsequent glaze compression being lost through the expansion of the body, due to absorption, for example.

Suggested remedies:

Either increase the degree of thermal expansion of the clay body by adding one of the forms of silica or decrease the thermal expansion of the glaze by adding China clay or silica.

UNFIRED GLAZE EXCESSIVELY FRAGILE

If a glaze film is extremely fragile it makes loading into the kiln, and handling in general, difficult. Either modify the glaze to include an increased clay content or add gum to the glaze.

GREENWARES EXCESSIVELY FRAGILE

Add a plasticizer – ball clay or bentonite – to the body formulation.

PEELING OF THE GLAZE FILM

The peeling of glaze away from the surfaces of a ceramic form most frequently occurs at a change of plane within the form. There are several possible causes:

1 Dust or dirt on the surface of the form causing poor glaze adhesion. Keep pots wrapped in paper after bisque firing if they are not to be glazed immediately.
2 Soluble salts within the clay body lifting the glaze film or preventing it from adhering to the form. Compound 2 per cent barium carbonate into the clay body.
3 Excessive compression strains between body and glaze. Lower silica content of the body or glaze as appropriate.

COLOUR STAINING OF GLAZES

Certain glaze colouring agents are volatile in the kiln and affect other wares around them – chromic oxide is particularly notorious in this respect.

DULL, DRY GLAZE SURFACE

Possible causes:

1 Insufficient silica in the glaze formulation.
2 Excessive reduction in firing (usually there is a black or grey discolouration in this case).
3 Glaze applied too thinly.
4 Glaze underfired.

GLAZE EXCESSIVELY FLUID

Glaze which runs down the form and possibly on to the kiln shelves may simply be the result of too thick an application of glaze to the ware or, more likely, over-firing. If this is not the case the glaze needs to be re-designed, but the addition of kaolin to the glaze may provide a simple solution.

CRAWLING

Crawling is the pulling apart of areas of glaze leaving parts of the form bald. The glaze also tends to form into globules on the clay surface.

The most common cause of crawling is grease on the surface of the bisque form from excessive handling of the pot. Alternatively, it may occur where underglaze decoration has been applied too thickly.)

If the glaze film cracks as it dries on the surface of the bisque and these fragments pull apart during firing to create crawling there is excessive shrinkage of glaze components and part of the clay content of the glaze should be replaced with calcined clay.

BLISTERING AND BUBBLING

Blistering and bubbling within the glaze are normally due to one of the following:

1 Overfiring.
2 Excessively fast glaze firing. Decrease the rate of temperature rise and allow the kiln to soak 30 to 60 minutes at maturation.
3 Glaze applied too thickly.
4 Glaze applied to an extremely porous form which has not been quenched in clean water.
5 Excessive use of body colourants, such as manganese dioxide, in the clay.

PINHOLES

Pinholing may result from glaze being applied to an excessively porous pot that has not been quenched before glazing. In this case pinholes frequently occur in the unfired glaze film also – these should be smoothed over with the fingers before being packed in the kiln.

Pinholing occurs during glaze firing when volatile gases leave the melting glaze and the kiln is not sufficiently soaked on maturation to allow them to heal over.

Pinholing, like other glaze defects, can also be the result of soluble sulphates being present in the clay (recognizable by a whitish deposit on the greenwares). Add 2 per cent barium carbonate to the body formulation.

Organic matter in glazes decomposes after the glazes have been made up for some considerable length of time. This can cause both bubbling and pinholing. Prepare and store glazes in a dry state and only make sufficient into slip form to satisfy a few weeks' requirements.

Toxicity

Lead and other heavy metals such as antimony, cadmium, selenium, barium and zinc are all toxic and can be detrimental to health if ingested. The danger of plumbism is particularly prevalent and great precaution is necessary in the use of raw lead chemicals.

Glazes containing lead are prone to attack from acids (particularly so when they are in combination with boron or when the glazes are under-fired) and care should be taken to avoid taking the following foodstuffs from lead glazed wares:

Vinegar (acetic acid)
Coffee (succinic acid)
Fruit juices (citric acid)
Apple juice (malic acid)

Whenever possible lead should be introduced into glazes in the safe form of a low solubility frit.

Plasterwork

Plaster is a material of great value to the potter, who uses it to make bats and moulds of various kinds – throwing bats for use on the wheel, drying bats for thickening slip, slurry or clay and moulds for slab work and all kinds of slip casting.

The mixing of plaster for use in industrial situations is a carefully regulated and controlled process, but when plaster is required for small scale use in the studio a much more simple and empirical technique is used.

One Imperial gallon of water normally requires 10 to 12 lb of potter's plaster to make a satisfactory mix (or 4·5 litres requires 4 to 5 kg). (Use more dense plaster mix for throwing bats and slightly less dense for drying bats.) This total will occupy a volume of approximately 300 cubic inches (5000 cc).

Weigh out the approximate amount of plaster that is required and pass it through a 30-mesh sieve to remove any lumps it may contain. Measure out the required volume of water and pour it into a large plastic container. Sprinkle the plaster evenly and slowly over the whole surface of the water, taking care that 'hills' of plaster do not protrude above the surface.

Add the whole amount of plaster to the water in this way; it should absorb all the water. If there is still a layer of clear water above the plaster it will eventually give rise to a soft and highly absorbent material and it is advisable to add more plaster until the excess water is absorbed. Leave the plaster to slake for three minutes, then mix the entire contents of the container to disperse any lumps which may have formed – this is best done by hand as you can then easily feel when the mixture has become homogenous. (Alternatively, a large perforated kitchen spoon or whisk can be used for mixing.)

After the mixing process is complete tap the sides of the plastic container gently. This will bring to the surface any bubbles of air held within the mixture.

Allow the plaster to stand undisturbed until it begins to thicken to a heavy creamy consistency. This is the first stage in setting and is the point when the plaster must be poured into the mould. Plaster usually takes about four minutes from the end of the mixing stage to thicken to the consistency at which it should be poured. Since plaster varies and since timing is critical, however, you should not rely too heavily on clock time but prefer to test the plaster empirically. A good test is to run your finger across the surface of the plaster; this will leave a trail behind it. Slap the sides of the container with your hand a few times gently. If the shock from this impact causes the surface of the plaster to smooth over and the trail to disappear you can afford to wait longer. Repeat this process until evidence of the trail remains on the surface, then pour the plaster at once.

As soon as the plaster has been poured wipe out the container with plenty of wet newspaper and discard into the garbage can. Never wash the remains of the mix down the sink. The advantage of a flexible container for mixing plaster is that should plaster be inadvertently allowed to set it can be easily removed by distorting the container, which will cause rigid plaster to crack and separate.

MAKING PLASTER BATS

The two most common types of plaster bat used in the studio are the large rectangular ones used as shelves in damp cupboards or for the drying of wet clay and the round ones used as throwing bats on the wheel. The latter should be made as dense as possible.

The rectangular bats can be made within a simple frame made from four lengths of wood sealed at the base and corners with clay or within a bat mould, which consists of wooden sides with a metal locking device at one end. This also must be sealed with clay at base and corners.

In either case the frame should be set up on a rigid polished surface such as a piece of marble, mirror or plate glass and both base and frame painted over with a coat of parting solution. Cheap and simple parting solutions may be made by dissolving paraffin wax in kerosene or by boiling 4 oz of grated laundry soap in 1½ pints of rain water until clear (200 g of soap in 1 litre of water).

The plaster may now be mixed and poured into the frame and left to

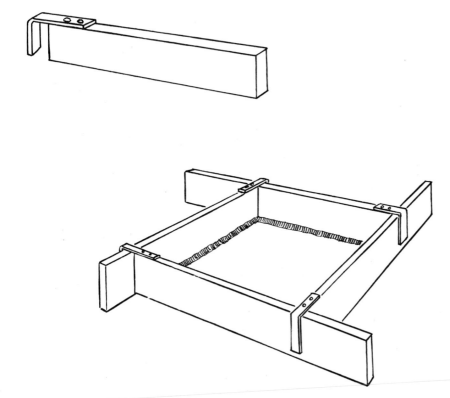

Adjustable mould for making plaster drying bats. Place the frame on a smooth firm surface and seal the join with a little plastic clay. Paint the inside of the frame and the base with parting solution before filling with plaster.

set. The frame may be removed after about an hour and the bat separated from the base. To accomplish this latter place a piece of wood along the longest edge of the bat and tap it gently with a wooden mallet.

Throwing bats are cast in metal bat moulds. Like the rectangular bats, they should be set up on a marble base and painted with parting solution. Seal these moulds with clay around their outside edge. In mixing plaster for throwing bats use as large a mass of plaster to each unit of water as is possible. The particularly hard and dense type of plaster known as 'Caffin D' is ideal for throwing bats.

It is essential that both faces of throwing bats should be perfectly plane. The face in contact with the marble presents no problems in this respect, but the upper face normally has to be scraped flat. This is most easily accomplished when the plaster has set to a stiff cheese-like consistency by scraping it down to the level of the metal mould with a metal straight edge.

The bat may be removed from the mould after an hour or so by placing a piece of flat wood across its surface and gently tapping it free with a mallet.

Glossary

AIR FLOATED Method of separating ceramic materials into particle sizes.

BALL MILL Device for grinding ceramic materials.

BANDING The application of a band of colour to a pot.

BAT Flat slab of fired clay, plaster, etc. on which pots are formed or clay is dried.

BISQUE Pottery which has had one firing preliminary to glazing.

BLUNGER Device for mixing clay slip.

CALCINE To heat a substance until it loses chemically combined water and volatile gases.

CLAY BODY A calculated composition of clays designed to satisfy specific working requirements.

CRAWLING Irregular firing of a glaze which leaves areas of the clay body bald.

CRAZE To develop fine cracks in a glaze film.

DAMPER Device for controlling chimney apertures in a kiln.

DUNT To split or shatter as a result of cooling.

ENGOBE A clay slip which is adjusted to suit the body to which it is to be applied.

FILLER A largely non-plastic material included in a clay body – usually siliceous.

FILTER PRESS Mechanical device for removing excess water from a clay slip.

FLASHING Surface discolouration by the effects of direct fire.

FLUX A clay or glaze component which promotes fusion and melt.

FRIT A group of ceramic materials which have been melted together, cooled and reground to powder form – used to eliminate undesirable qualities such as toxicity or solubility.

FUDE Round pointed Japanese brush.

GLOST FIRE Glaze fire.

GREENWARE Unfired pottery forms.

GROG Fired and reground refractory clay.

HAKE Flat Japanese brush.

LAWN Screen or sieve.

LEATHER HARD Clay ware that has been partially dried and in which shrinkage is virtually complete.

LUTE Method of joining slabs of leather-hard clay by using clay slip.

MATURE Fired so that it becomes a tight structure.

MISHIMA Decoration of contrasting coloured clay inlaid into a clay form.

NERITAGE Japanese process of forming pots by combining clays of two different colours.

OPEN To make a clay body more porous.

PADDLE Flat wooden tool used to shape pots or to mix clay slip.

P.C.E. Pyrometric cone equivalent

PEELING The separation of a slip or glaze from the body.

PLASTIC Malleable.

PLASTICITY The ability of a clay to be modelled into a form and to retain that shape upon drying.

PUG A mechanical means of mixing clay.

PYROMETER Device for measuring kiln temperatures.

PYROMETRIC CONE Device for measuring the effects of heat in a kiln.

REDUCTION FIRE A kiln atmosphere deficient in oxygen.

REFRACTORY Resistant to the effects of heat.

SAGGAR A fireclay box which contains pots during firing.

SEDIMENTARY Deposited in strata.

SGRAFFITO Decoration by scratching and incising into surfaces.

SINTER Fire to the point where the material begins to melt.

SLAKE To saturate with water.

SLIP Clay or glaze particles evenly suspended in water.

SLURRY An unrefined mixture of clay and water.

SOAK To maintain a kiln temperature at a given level.

SPRIGGING Joining bas relief decoration on to a pottery form.

SPURS Refractory props which support wares during firing.

THERMAL SHOCK Severe stresses in a ceramic form caused by sudden changes in temperature.

THERMOCOUPLE The thermal sensor of a pyrometer.

THROW To form articles on the potter's wheel.

TOOTH A degree of coarseness in a clay body.

VITRIFY To fire to the point where glass is formed.

WEDGE To mix clay by cutting and kneading.

Bibliography

Reference Books

BECK, C. *Stoneware Glazes* Burnley, England: Isles House Publications 1973

BILLINGTON, D. M. *Technique of Pottery* London: Batsford 1962

CARDEW, M. *Pioneer Pottery* London: Longman 1969

DICKERSON, J. *Raku Handbook* London: Studio Vista; New York: Van Nostrand Reinhold 1972

DODD, A. E. *Dictionary of Ceramics* London: Newnes; New Jersey: Littlefield, Adams & Co. 1967

FRASER, H. *Glazes for the Craft Potter* London: Pitman; New York: Watson-Guptill 1973

FOURNIER, ROBERT *An Illustrated Dictionary of Practical Pottery* London and New York: Van Nostrand Reinhold 1974

LAWRENCE, W. G. *Ceramic Science for the Potter* Philadelphia: Chilton 1972

LEACH, B. *A Potter's Book* London: Faber & Faber; New York: Transatlantic Arts 1945

NELSON, G. C. *Ceramics – A Potter's Handbook* New York: Holt, Rinehart & Winston 1960

PARMELEE, C. W. *Ceramic Glazes* Boston: Industrial Publications 1951

RHODES, D. *Clay and Glazes for the Potter* Philadelphia: Chilton 1957; London: Pitman 1958

RHODES, D. *Stoneware and Porcelain* London: Pitman; Philadelphia: Chilton 1959

RHODES, D. *Kilns: Design, Construction and Operation* London: Pitman; Philadelphia: Chilton 1970

WORALL, W. E. *Clays: Their Nature, Origin and General Properties* London: Applied Science Publication 1968

Periodicals

Dansk Kunsthaandvaerk: Copenhagen, Denmark

La Ceramica: Milan, Italy   out 9 print.

Vrienden van de Nederlandse Ceramik: Amsterdam, The Netherlands

Pottery in Australia: Turramurra, N.S.W., Australia

Ceramic Review: London, England

Ceramics Monthly: Columbus, Ohio, U.S.A.

Craft Horizons: New York, U.S.A.

Pottery Quarterly: Tring, England

Ceramic Data Books: Industrial Publications, Chicago, Ill., U.S.A.

Suppliers of ceramic materials

Australia

CERAMIC ART SUPPLIES 53 Pulteney Street, Adelaide 5000

CERAMIC SUPPLY CO. 61 Lakemba Street, Belmore, N.S.W. 2192

HARRISON & CROSFIELD (ANZ) LTD 17-27 Newstead Ave, Newstead, Brisbane, Queensland

HARRISON & CROSFIELD (ANZ) LTD 331 Murray Street, Perth, Western Australia

POTTERS' WORKSHOP 28 Greenaway Street, Bulleen, Victoria 3105

RODDA & CO. (SA) PTY LTD Eastern Parade, Rosewater, South Australia

RUSSELL COWAN PTY LTD 136 Pacific Highway, Waitara, N.S.W. 2077

SOUTH AUSTRALIAN STUDIO POTTERS' CLUB INC. 16 Sussex Street, North Adelaide 5006

WALKER CERAMICS Boronia Road, Watsonia, Victoria 3087

Canada

BAROID OF CANADA LTD 5108 Eighth Avenue S.W., Calgary, Alberta

BARRETT CO. LTD 1155 Dorchester Blvd, W. Montreal 2, P.Q.

BLYTHE COLORS LTD Toronto, Ontario

CLAYBURN HARBISON LTD 1690 West Broadway, Vancouver, British Columbia

GREATER TORONTO CERAMIC CENTRE 167 Lakeshore Road, Toronto 14, Ontario

A. P. GREEN FIREBRICK CO. Rosemount Avenue, Weston, Ontario

MERCEDES CERAMIC SUPPLY 8 Wallace Street, Woodbridge, Ontario

POTTERY SUPPLY HOUSE 491 Wildwood Road, Oakville, Ontario

SASKATCHEWAN CLAY PRODUCTS Box 970, Estevan, Saskatchewan

England

BRITISH CERAMIC SERVICE CO. LTD Bricesco House, 1 Park Avenue, Wolstanton, Newcastle, Staffs

FULHAM POTTERY 210 New Kings Road, London SW6

COLIN PEARSON & DENNIS HEALING The Firs, Marston Magna, Yeovil, Somerset (for the 'Rapid Ceramic Glaze Calculator')

PIKE BROS Wareham, Dorset

W. PODMORE & SONS LTD Caledonia Mills, Shelton, Stoke-on-Trent, Staffs

POTCLAYS LTD Wharf House, Copeland Street, Hanley, Stoke-on-Trent, Staffs

ALEX TIRANTI LTD 73 Charlotte Street, London W1

WENGERS LTD Etruria, Stoke-on-Trent, Staffs

New Zealand

CLIVE POTTERY STUDIO 203 Parnell Road, Auckland 1

A. C. EMERY 14 Kohimarama Road, Auckland 5

ALLAN HEDGER 94 Federal Street, Auckland 1

RIVERSIDE POTTERIES R. D. 2 Amberley, Christchurch

TITAN POTTERY LTD Great South Road, Takanini

U.S.A.

ALASKA MUD PUDDLE 9034 Hartzell Road, Anchorage, Alaska 99502

AMERICAN ART CLAY CO. 4717 W. 16 Street, Indianapolis, Indiana 46222

CAPITAL CERAMICS 2174 S. Main Street, Salt Lake City, Utah 84115

CEDAR HEIGHTS CLAY CO. Oak Hill, Ohio 45656

CERAMIC COLOR & CHEMICAL MANUFACTURING CO. Box 297, New Brighton Pennsylvania 15066

CERAMICS-HAWAII LTD 629 Cooke Street, Honolulu, Hawaii 96813

DFC CERAMICS 2401 East 40th Ave., Denver, Colorado 80205

FERRO CORPORATION 4150 East 56th Street, Cleveland, Ohio 44105

GENERAL REFRACTORIES CO. 7640 West Chicago Ave., Detroit, Michigan 48204

HAMMILL & GILLESPIE INC. 255 Broadway, New York, N.Y. 10007

O. HOMMEL CO. Hope Street, Carnegie, Pennsylvania 15106

PEMCO CORPORATION 5601 Eastern Ave., Baltimore, Maryland 21202

STANDARD CERAMIC SUPPLY CO. Box 4435, Pittsburgh, Pennsylvania 15205

TERRA CERAMICS 3035 Koapako Street, Honolulu, Hawaii 96819

VAN HOWE CERAMIC SUPPLY CO. 4216 Edith N.E., Albuquerque, New Mexico 87107

WESTERN CERAMICS SUPPLY CO. 1601 Howard Street, San Francisco, California 94103

Index